Building Reading Comprehension

High-Interest Selections for Critical Reading Skills

Linda Piazza

illustrated by Linda Pierce

cover by Matthew Van Zomeren

Publisher
Instructional Fair • TS Denison
Grand Rapids, Michigan 49544

To the Teacher

This book addresses reading comprehension skills through informational, practical, persuasive, and fictional readings. The activities that accompany each selection focus on specific skills, which are identified in the table of contents. They require students to think, to be creative, and to be attentive to the details and directions that are included.

Skills covered include drawing conclusions; identifying sources; determining fact and opinion; comparing and contrasting; examining the writer's purpose; drawing inferences; reading directions; drawing conclusions; working with concept maps, words in context, and sequence of events; identifying conflict; reading graphs, floor plans, and maps; and identifying stereotypes.

These high-interest readings reflect students' current interests and their experiences. They read about creepy robots to study the writer's purpose. They must pay attention to detail when decoding beeper messages and making a mystery origami project, and they must read a school's floor plan to solve a crime. They answer a survey and compare and contrast their own answers to those of actual teen respondents.

Choose those pages that meet the needs of your students. And most important of all, give your students time to enjoy their reading!

ISBN: 1-56822-915-1
Reading Comprehension: Grades 7-8
Copyright © 2000 by Instructional Fair Group
a Tribune Education Company
3195 Wilson Dr. NW
Grand Rapids, Michigan 49544

All Rights Reserved • Printed in the USA

Table of Contents

Epidemic

A deadly virus struck three middle school students on the same day. To stop the virus, health officials have to find out where they were exposed. Each student attends a different school, so when were they all together in one place?

Fortunately, each of them kept a diary, planner, or calendar. Read their entries; then follow the directions to document when they were exposed.

Rochelle

What a day! First I slept late and almost missed practice for Texas Lone Star cheerleaders. At the end of practice, though, Sean told me that he liked my attitude! I kept smiling all through practice for Houston Children's Chorus. When I went to the football game that night, I kept imagining being down there cheering. But for Cy-Falls, not Cy-Springs or Langham!

Weston

Saturday

8:00   Breakfast at Denny's. Meet Brittany there. Go to Cy-Springs together. Set up our experiments by 9:30 for the judges.

2:00   Practice with HCC for the fall program.

6:30   Be ready to go to the game if I want a ride with Greg. Bring video camera so I can film Greg's winning touchdown against Langham! Or his big fumble!

Brittany's Grateful Journal

Today I'm grateful that

1. I didn't place high enough at the science fair to go on to state! Let Weston go. He's got a cool physical science teacher at his school.
2. Mom and Weston's mom still like each other from when we used to live in the same neighborhood. They talked so much they forgot to ask us all those dopey questions parents ask when they were driving us around every place.
3. I didn't break my leg at soccer practice today when I ran Ashley down going after the ball, and I didn't break Ashley's leg either.
4. Langham won!
5. No practices and no homework tomorrow!

Below is a Venn diagram. Each circle represents the activities of one of the three students. The areas where the circles overlap represent activities two or more students share. Below is a list of the activities the researchers compiled after reading the passages on the previous page. Put them in the correct areas of the circles. You do not have to be certain whether the students participated in a particular activity, if there is evidence that they might have participated. The goal is to find a place or places where they all might have been together. The activity or activities in which all three participated will be placed in the shape formed where all three circles overlap.

Activities:

Texas Star soccer practice
Breakfast at Denny's
Science Fair at Langham Creek
Cy-Springs/Langham Creek football game
Texas Lone Star cheerleaders' practice
Houston Children's Chorus practice

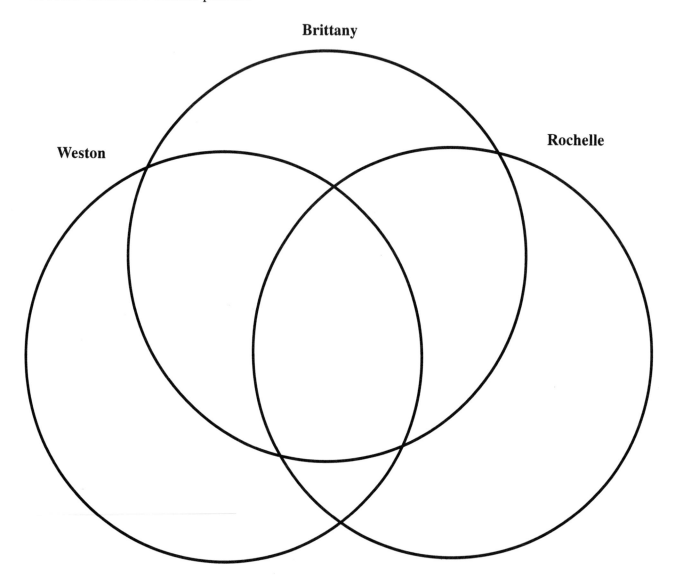

What's It All About?

A classmate wants to know what a book is about. You launch into a description of the book's plot and explain to the classmate what happens. A book is also about the theme being developed. The theme tells what the author wants readers to learn. "People matter more than things" might be the theme of a story or book, for example. Often themes can be expressed in the form of familiar folk sayings or proverbs. Below you will find a list that contains brief descriptions of Newbery Award-winning books. You will find another list of proverbs that might be the themes of books. Match the books to the proverbs which might describe their themes. Some proverbs will not be used. Write the proverb that goes with each book.

1. In *A Girl Named Disaster* by Nancy Farmer, readers discover a riveting adventure tale. This book features an 11-year-old Mozambique villager. She sets out to find her father in Zimbabwe. Along the way, she comforts herself with the stories and memories she carries in her heart. _____

2. Eloise McGraw's *Moorchild* introduces a main character who is half-human and half-Folk. Considered an outcast in both worlds, she must come to terms with being and looking different. _____

3. Gen boasts, lies, and scams his way through Megan Whalen Turner's *The Thief*. He can't be believed. He fools his captors, and perhaps readers, too! _____

4. Palmer LaRue has a secret. He is sheltering a pigeon from the town's pigeon-shoot fund-raiser. Bullies pursue Palmer and the pigeon, too, in Jerry Spinelli's *Wringer*. Will Palmer take a stand against the bullies? Traditionally, the town recruits boys Palmer's age to wring the necks of the wounded pigeons. Will Palmer take a stand against that, too? _____

PROVERBS

Believe only half of what you see and nothing that you hear.
Beauty is in the eye of the beholder.
Still waters run deep.
He who fights and runs away may live to fight another day.
He who lies down with the dogs will rise with fleas.
Home is where the heart is.
Don't count your chickens before they hatch.
A wise man changes his mind; a fool never will.
Half a loaf is better than none.

☞ Words have been omitted from the selection below, and two alternates have been suggested. Scan the selection and think about the main idea. Then look at the choices offered for each word. With that main idea in mind, circle the one that best fits the context of the article.

We All Know Lucy, But Who Are Madelyn and Bob?

Lucy, Ricky, Fred, and Ethel. Anyone who cruises late-night television, remote control in hand, is familiar with these characters featured in the '50s television sitcom *I Love Lucy*. What about Madelyn and Bob? Does anyone know their names?

Madelyn Pugh and Bob Carroll, Jr., wrote every scene in all 180 episodes of *I Love Lucy*. The show premiered in October of 1951, but Pugh and Carroll had been a (writing/acting) team for years by then. They continued with the show until its final (chapter/episode) at the close of the 1956-1957 television season.

Although their names might not be (recognizable/pronounceable), people know more about Pugh's and Carroll's lives than they might imagine. Pugh and Carroll based many episodes on events in their own lives. Each episode of the (radio program/sitcom) usually began with an ordinary premise, then escalated into a (funny/predictable) situation. Many of those ordinary premises were prompted by something that had (seemed funny/happened) to Pugh or Carroll. Carroll talked about one day when he and Pugh were lunching with a friend at the Derby restaurant. Every time one of the two men mentioned what they wanted to order, Pugh would change her own (order/hat). Pugh and Carroll opened the episode "Lucy Changes Her Mind" with a similar (scene/hat).

If you watch reruns of contemporary sitcoms such as *The Nanny* and *Roseanne*, you might spy episodes that recreate favorite *I Love Lucy* scenes. Did Pugh and Carroll have any idea they were creating shows that would become classics? No, says Pugh in an interview with David Martindale for the *Houston Chronicle*.

Do Pugh and Carroll wish that the public understood their (donation/contribution) to the popular series? Maybe they do, but both also believe that the stars of the show (deserved/craved) the credit they have been given. Lucy was willing to do whatever the script called for her to do. Her willingness and talent and that of the other stars made Pugh's and Carroll's words live and go on living through the decades.

Help on the Internet

You and your friends are sprawled in a circle around a pile of textbooks and wadded-up papers. "We need help," someone finally says.

Help may be as close as your computer. Internet sites offer reference materials, homework help, and advice in finding specialized information. A site offering profiles of famous people will not help you with a math problem, though. Match the homework assignments with the Internet sites likely to contain the help you need.

Site 1: http://www.tiua.edu/american_studies/spring_98_classes/~coast-cascades98/references/research_paper/research_paper.htm offers help for everything from choosing a topic to citing your sources. This source updates the information each year, so you might try substituting the last two numbers of the current year for the places where you see 98 in this URL.

Site 2: http://www.english.upenn.edu/~jlynch/grammar.html can help you decide when to use a semicolon and when to use a colon. You can get help with other grammar-related issues here, too.

Site 3: http://indy4.fdl.cc.mn.us/~isk/stories/myths.html includes a collection of American Indian myths, stories, and legends.

Site 4: http://www.megaconverter.com converts weights and measures to metric and back again.

Site 5: http://www.homeworkcentral.com serves as a clearinghouse which funnels you to the right site for academic help. Real people track down the academic sites you need.

Site 6: http://www.askanexpert.com/askanexpert connects you to experts in various fields. Select the category that interests you. You will be presented with a list of experts in that field. Choose one, and then check the expert's web site. You may find your answer on the expert's web site. If not, you can e-mail the expert to ask your questions.

Site 7: http://www.writes.org/netscape/literature_net/index.html lists novels available on the Internet. Some are even illustrated, such as Dickens's *A Christmas Carol* and Lewis Carroll's *Through the Looking Glass*.

Name _____

Answer the questions below.

1. Not fair! Your physical science teacher assigned a research paper on a famous discovery. You know what topic you want, and you even found a lot of information on the Internet, saving you a trip to the library. Now at the last moment, you remember that you were supposed to interview someone and include a quotation. To save your grade-point average, which site would you type on your keyboard? _____

   _____

2. Uh-oh! The good news is that you are almost over the flu and can probably go back to school tomorrow. The bad news is that you just remembered that by tomorrow you are supposed to know where a certain country is located. You think it is on the African continent, but you are not certain. Your parents will not get off work in time to take you to the library to look at the atlas. You could look it up now, if you knew whether there were any atlases on-line. To find out if there are any atlases, which Internet resource would you check? _____

   _____

3. Hmm. Your language arts teacher has asked you to write a new ending for a traditional story or tale. Everyone else writes new endings for *Three Little Pigs* and other familiar stories, but you have never been like anyone else. You want something different. Which site would you check first? _____

   _____

4. Quotation quotas. You got ten points off your last book report because you put quotation marks around the title of the book every time you mentioned it. Now the book you want to review is a collection of short stories. Help! When do you underline and when do you use quotation marks? To find out, which two sources could you check? _____

   _____

5. Too much! You have too much to do. You keep forgetting things. One Sunday evening when you have just settled down, you remember that your language arts teacher had given your class a list of classic novels. You were supposed to have chosen one by Monday and filled out a paper listing the main character and some other details about the first chapter. You have lots of books at your house, but they are mostly medical thrillers. How can you find and read the first chapter of a classic novel? _____

   _____

☞ Taking effective notes can help you recall material more easily. Some students find that concept maps help them visualize material and also see how the details relate to one another. Related ideas are connected to one another by a ray or line. A concept map begins with a single word or phrase that tells the main topic being discussed. The main topic being discussed in this selection is the causes of lightning. This topic is enclosed in a circle on the following page. As you scan the article, jot down other important concepts and ideas. Draw lines that connect related ideas.

Hunting the Causes of Lightning

The plane bucks, metal groaning. Up front, pilot and copilot frown, studying the instrument panel. In back, researchers study other instruments, but the researchers are smiling. They are hunting down storms that might produce lightning, and they have just found one.

More than 200 years after Benjamin Franklin flew a kite into a lightning storm, scientists still are not certain what causes lightning. Studies conducted on spring nights over the skies of the Great Plains states may help them find the causes. On spring nights, cool air converges with warmer air, triggering the storms that produce lightning.

One theory states that a bigger bit of ice slams into a smaller bit of ice, leaving behind a positive or negative charge. The larger the bit of ice and the faster it is going, the bigger the charge it leaves behind. When enough of these charges collect, lightning occurs. Scientists with the National Oceanic and Atmospheric Administration measure the size of the particles, their speed, wind speed, temperature, and air pressure, looking for the right combination that tends to produce lightning. Making these measurements requires that pilots fly alongside the storms. Sometimes the storm moves unpredictably, so that pilots find themselves flying into the storm rather than skirting it.

In the spring of 1998, scientists uncovered another clue that may help unravel the causes of lightning. That spring, smoke from massive Mexican fires drifted over the south-central United States. Texas, Oklahoma, Colorado, and Nebraska were most affected. In those same areas, a strange phenomenon was noted. Between 60 and 70 percent of the lightning strikes proved to be positively charged. Usually, about 90 percent of lightning strikes are negatively charged. Walter Lyons, an atmospheric scientist with the Colorado firm FMA, Inc., commented that this strange behavior warns that scientists still do not understand what causes lightning.

Why is it important to know what causes lightning? Lightning causes fires and electrical damage, especially positively charged lightning such as that noted in the spring of 1998. Lightning is the number one storm-related killer in the United States. Statistics compiled by the National Weather Service indicate that each year more people are killed by lightning than by tornadoes and hurricanes combined. The first step in preventing those deaths is to understand what produces lightning.

CAUSES OF LIGHTNING

Now do not refer to the article and answer the following questions.

1. Some scientists are studying ice particles in storms to determine whether they could cause lightning. They measure their size, their speed, and the wind speed. What else do they measure? _____

2. Which states were affected by the smoke drifting up from Mexico? _____

   _____

3. Name two reasons it is important to study the causes of lightning. _____

   _____

   _____

4. After the smoke from Mexican fires drifted over the south-central United States, what percentage of the lightning strikes were positively charged? _____

   _____

Name _____

You Recognize This Person, Don't You?

A new student knocks at the classroom door, flashes a grin at the student aide who walked her to the class, then saunters into the classroom. Her blonde hair brushes her shoulders.

You already have an idea whether she is someone you want to know. Her appearance, her manner of moving, and her actions have given you clues about her personality.

Writers use some of these same clues to characterize the people who appear in their stories. Read the passages that follow and match them with the character sketches.

Passage 1:
Ashley sat beneath the oak, her hands clasped over her blue-jeaned knees and her face turned up into the dappled light. "Fall is my favorite time of year," she whispered.

Passage 2:
Tricia grimaced as she pressed the bar up the last time, then let it drop with a clang into the hooks on either side of the bench press. As she sat up, she wiped a fine sheen of sweat from her forehead, then grinned. "That's the most I've ever done," she said.

Passage 3:
Sean pinched the bridge of his nose and sighed heavily. He leaned forward again over his opened book, his elbows on the table and his hands supporting his forehead.

Write 1, 2, or 3:

_____ This character's primary trait is persistence. Sometimes this character spends so much time making decisions, opportunities are lost.

_____ This character is often offered unsolicited advice, as others don't see the strong will and determination beneath this character's quiet manner.

_____ Cheerful and exuberant, this character likes to be the center of attention. This character is a hard worker, but will drop an activity that isn't any fun.

☞ In a persuasive essay, some statements are debatable. People might agree or disagree with debatable statements. They are not fact. The goal of the writer is to persuade readers to agree with these debatable statements. To persuade readers, the writer includes support for the arguments. Those supporting statements can be statements of fact. Facts are nondebatable. Everyone agrees that they are true. Read the essay and then answer the questions about the debatable and nondebatable statements.

Ban Oxygen on Everest

In the first 74 years of assaults on Everest, 144 lives were lost, an average of less than two lives a year. In a single climbing season in the late '90s, 12 people perished in their attempts to climb Everest. The increasing commercialization of Everest can be blamed. Guides and Sherpas charge fees in the tens of thousands of dollars. For these fees, they haul climbers of questionable skills up and down the mountain. Without supplemental oxygen, these climbers would probably collapse at the lower, safer levels. With supplemental oxygen, they climb higher.

Ban oxygen canisters from the summit, except for emergencies, and the problem is solved. Accomplished mountaineers in supreme physical condition would still be able to reach the summit. Less-accomplished mountaineers would be forced to turn back at lower levels. Those caught in storms or experiencing medical problems would be more accessible to help. If supplementary oxygen allows them to climb beyond their natural physical limits, rescuers lives are risked, too.

This ban would have another benefit. It would eliminate the scandalous littering of the world's most famous mountain with discarded oxygen canisters. The Sherpas call Everest Mother Goddess of the Earth. Are spent oxygen canisters and the dead bodies of paying clients fitting ornaments for her to wear?

Circle N(ondebatable) or D(ebatable):

N   D   1. Twelve people died on Everest in one climbing season.

N   D   2. The increasing commercialization of Everest contributed to the number of deaths.

N   D   3. Mount Everest is littered with discarded oxygen canisters.

N   D   4. Accomplished mountaineers in supreme physical condition would be able to climb Mount Everest without supplemental oxygen.

☞ Characters in stories and books can inspire readers to try new things or overcome obstacles. This happens when readers identify with a character who struggles and succeeds. That character is changed in some way at the end of the story. Readers believe they might succeed in the same way. The character has experienced character growth, and perhaps readers can, too. Read the following story, thinking about the main character's problem. Notice how she struggles. Then answer the questions that follow.

One Step at a Time

Tracy studied the girls ahead of her, numbers pinned to each hunter-green shirt. Tracy's was kelly green.

She bit her lip. "Don't worry about everything all at once," her grandmother always told her. "Break each problem into little steps."

How? No way was she going to be able to smile. Her back tucks had been so low yesterday that she'd landed on her knees. She'd been chanting too fast all week.

One step at a time, she told herself, but her chest tightened.

The gym door opened, and a girl slipped inside. Tracy heard a faint "Go, Eagles!" What if she started before the judges gave her the signal?

She shook her head. Worry about the tumbling.

Impossible to break even that into separate steps. She had to get her timing right, keep her feet together, remember not to make duck hands.

She moaned, stepping out of line.

"Where are you going?" the girl behind her said. "You're next."

Next?

The gym door opened. The girl pushed Tracy inside.

The judges sat at a table all the way across the polished gym floor.

Tracy swallowed. She was going to throw up. She was going to faint.

All those faces watching. All that distance to go.

She let her breath out in a long hiss, then took off. Halfway into her hurdle, she remembered that she hadn't yelled, hadn't made any hand signals.

She pitched forward, then caught herself. Her heart thundered, and she couldn't move. Just go forward, she told herself. Just take the first step.

On the second flip-flop, she realized she was rebounding high enough. She hurled herself through the back tuck, landing on both feet.

She grinned, yelled "Go, Eagles," then ran forward. One step at a time.

Write your answers.

1. Why is Tracy standing in line at the beginning of the story? _____

   _____

2. What is there about Tracy's personality that might make it harder for her to succeed in these tryouts than it might be for other people? _____

   _____

   _____

Circle the correct answer.

3. A character's main or external conflict is the big problem that character has to overcome. A character's inner or internal conflict is the trait or fear that is going to make it harder for this character to overcome the main problem. Below are two conflicts. One is Tracy's main conflict and one is her inner conflict. Circle the one that is Tracy's inner conflict.

   Tracy is trying out for cheerleader.

   Tracy has trouble breaking big projects into little steps.

4. A character's inner or internal conflict makes it harder for that character to overcome the main conflict. Circle the sentences in which she has to remind herself to take one step at a time.

Write your answer.

5. At the end of the story, does Tracy learn to break big projects into one step at a time? _____ What evidence leads you to draw this conclusion? _____

   _____

6. Does the writer tell you whether Tracy makes cheerleader? _____ Would you guess that the writer feels that it is more important to say something about being a cheerleader or to say something about learning to break big projects into small steps? _____

   _____

Curfew Contract

You hurtle down the stairs as your best friend's mother pulls into your driveway. "The movie is over at 11:30," you call to your parents. "I should be home by 12:15."

But your parents are not in the den watching television as you thought. They are standing at the front door, and they hand you the following contract. Read it and answer the questions that follow.

Agreement

This agreement is entered into this _____ day of _____, by and between _____ and _____ hereinafter referred to as "Parents" and _____ hereinafter referred to as "Child."

Whereas, Child desires to be allowed to stay out until 12:00 midnight on weekends;

Whereas, Parents and Child agree that a curfew should be imposed;

Whereas, the parties hereto mutually agree, subject to the terms, conditions, and benefits herein, as follows:

1. Term: This Agreement shall be for a term of one year commencing _____.

2. Curfew Hours: Child shall be home by the following times:

Friday:	12:00 midnight
Saturday:	12:00 midnight
Sunday:	10:00 p.m.
Monday–Thursday:	9:00 p.m.

3. Violations: In the event of any violations of curfew by Child, Child hereby agrees that Parents may impose the following curfew actions:

   (a) Child will water and feed dog for one week for each violation.

   (b) In the event of two curfew violations during any one-week period, in addition to the curfew action set forth in (a) above, Child will cut grass, wash dinner dishes, wash all clothes, clean room, and cook breakfast for Parents for two weeks.

   (c) Watching TV shall be restricted to 30 minutes per day during the curfew action periods set forth in (a) or (b).

   (d) Three or more curfew violations during any one calendar month shall result in restriction to house for one month.

   Executed this _____ day of _____.

   _____
   Child

   _____
   Parent

You have no choice. You sign the contract. To signal that you understand the contract, fill in the appropriate blanks. You disagree with the phrase "Whereas, Parents *and Child* agree that a curfew should be imposed." To legally indicate your disagreement, cross out the words *and Child* in that line, then write your initials in the margin to the side of that line. Now answer the following Yes/No questions to see if you understand the terms of the contract you have signed.

Y   N   1.   You come in at 9:30 Sunday evening. Will you be subject to the curfew action set out in 3(a)?

Y   N   2.   You come in at 9:30 the next Tuesday evening. Will you be subject to the curfew action set out in 3(b) if you have not been late any other night that week?

Y   N   3.   You come in at 10:10 the next Sunday evening. Will you be subject to the curfew action set out in 3(c)?

Y   N   4.   If you come in at 8:50 the next Monday evening, will you be subject to the curfew action set out in 3(c)?

Y   N   5.   Will you be subject to the curfew action set out in 3(b)?

Y   N   6.   Look at the following list. Using this schedule as your guide, and considering that you have not been late any other nights in the preceding month, would you be subject to curfew action 3(d)? Remember to pay attention to the term "calendar month."

Sunday, October 30—Arrive home at 10:30 p.m.
Monday, October 31—Arrive home at 9:10 p.m.
Tuesday, November 1 —Arrive home at 8:30 p.m.
Wednesday, November 2—Arrive home at 6:30 p.m.
Thursday, November 3—Arrive home at 3:30 p.m.
Friday, November 4—Arrive home at 12:05 a.m.

Scientists Take Aim with AImS Camera

What do skin cancer, the star-spangled banner (the U.S. flag), Martian rocks, and prehistoric archeological sites all have in common? An infrared camera developed by NASA. John Hillman of NASA's Goddard Space Flight Center suggests that the camera might be used to detect skin cancer or locate minerals in Martian rocks. It might be used to analyze prehistoric sites.

Developed by Dr. David Glenar at Goddard, the Acousto-Optic Imaging Spectrometer (AImS) works differently than most infrared cameras. Most infrared cameras detect light emitted from an object due to its heat. The AImS camera detects differences in the way infrared light is reflected from different kinds of materials. It does not rely on difference in temperatures.

That was important to Suzanne Thomassen-Krauss, the restoration curator for The Star-Spangled Banner Project. She knew that the contaminants on the flag would be the same temperature as the wool cloth which made up the flag. In the late '90s the AImS camera was put to work finding those contaminants. Finding them was important. The flag flew over Baltimore's Fort McHenry in the War of 1812. It inspired the national anthem Francis Scott Key wrote two years later. Although the curators at the Smithsonian Institution's National Museum of American History had taken great care to protect the flag, it was deteriorating. In the presence of light, any moisture that collected on the flag caused a chemical reaction that deteriorated the wool. Dirt and oil also caused damage. It was not always possible to detect these contaminants with the human eye.

Hillman feels great pride that a camera developed in the Goddard Center could be used to help preserve a historic artifact. He looks forward to other uses being found for the camera.

Write your answers.

1. Who is the source of the information about why the Smithsonian Institution chose the AImS camera to help restorers work on The Star-Spangled Banner Project?

   _____

2. Who is the source of the information about the many ways the AImS camera might be used in the future?_____
   Circle the correct answer: This person probably has more expertise in . . .

   the medical field   restoration of artifacts   space technology   archeology

3. When John Hillman says that the AImS camera may be used to detect skin cancer, is he speculating or is he speaking as someone developing the technique to use the camera in this manner? _____
   What evidence do you have to support your conclusion? _____

They're Doing What?

Sometimes you can make inferences based on what you see in a photograph. The conclusions you make can influence your opinion about people, events, or developments. Study the photo below, and then write your answer to the questions that follow.

1. The performer leading the line is probably
    _____.
    a. a Native American
    b. a Mayan from the Yucatan
    c. a West African

2. This performance probably takes place on
    a _____.
    a. cold January day
    b. crisp autumn day
    c. hot July afternoon

3. The two tallest people following the
    performer are probably _____.
    a. the two tallest girls in this group
    b. adults who broke in line
    c. adults who are chaperoning the group

4. This event is probably taking place ____.
    a. somewhere in the continental United
        States
    b. on the West African Plains
    c. somewhere in the Yucatan

5. These children probably are _____.
    a. being initiated into a secret society
    b. learning about another culture
    c. showing the performer a popular
        line dance

6. Most people looking at this photograph
    would conclude _____.
    a. that students should not be forced to
        go on field trips
    b. that learning about another culture
        can be a frightening experience
    c. that learning about this performer's
        culture was fun for the participants

☞ Tension is an important element in fiction. Tension draws readers through a story. Read this story, and then follow the directions to identify the ways the author builds tension.

Standing My Ground

"Ask her, Cory," Justin said, elbowing me. "Maybe they just forgot to send you the letter."

I shook my head and bent to stuff my math book and papers into my backpack.

"Maybe it got lost," Justin said.

I zipped my backpack. "Your parents got the letter inviting you to the pre-algebra class more than a week ago. They just don't want me in next year's honors class—the same way coach never wants me in the soccer game."

"That one's easy," Justin said. "You've got the skill. You just don't want the ball bad enough."

I shrugged.

"Hey, I gotta go," Justin called over his shoulder. "See you last period."

Some people were gathered around Mrs. Irani, asking her about their grades. She didn't change any, I noticed.

When the last person left, Mrs. Irani looked up. "Surely you don't want to complain about your grade?" she asked with a smile.

I felt my face flush. "No, ma'am," I said. I'd made another A, but all my A's hadn't been enough to get me a recommendation.

It was lunch period, and the hall was emptying, too. I could talk to Mrs. Irani, and nobody would know.

Mrs. Irani had picked up her books and her classroom keys. She walked to the door; then she turned to look at me again.

"I was wondering," I said.

"Wondering what?" she asked, jiggling her keys.

My mouth was so dry, my lips were sticking to my teeth. It was no use anyway. It was just that I'd thought I was good at math. I'd kind of thought maybe some day I'd be good at engineering or something like that.

"Nothing," I said, slipping the strap of my backpack over my shoulder. I'd probably bombed the math section of the TAAS test or something dumb like that. Or maybe Mrs. Irani could tell by the way I worked out my problems that I wouldn't be good at algebra.

I slipped past Mrs. Irani and turned toward the cafeteria. My heavy footsteps echoed in the nearly empty hall. Behind me, I heard her turn the key in the lock.

I stopped, my heart pounding. "Mrs. Irani?" I asked, turning toward her.

She lifted her eyebrows.

"I was wondering," I stammered, "why I wasn't recommended for the honors math class."

Mrs. Irani's brows lowered, and the corners of her mouth turned down. "That honors class is a tough one," she said. "It requires a teacher's recommendation, and I'm afraid I couldn't give you one."

My palms were damp. I crossed my arms and tucked my hands into my armpits. Now she was going to be giving me those sorry-you-couldn't-cut-it looks.

"We have to feel comfortable that students can ask for help when they need it, and I wasn't sure you would do that. You never participate in class."

"That's not fair," I blurted out. My heart felt like it was going to bust a rib. "I'm sorry for sounding so rude, but that isn't fair," I said. "I never needed help. I'd ask for it if I needed it."

Mrs. Irani's eyebrows went up again, way up underneath her bangs. She poked her lips out.

I took a deep breath and stood my ground.

Mrs. Irani laughed. "I can see you would ask for something if you needed it," she said. "No promises, but I'll talk to the head of the math department. Your grades are certainly good enough."

I grinned, but then wiped the grin away. "Yes, ma'am, they are," I said. "And thanks."

Mrs. Irani laughed again. "Go to lunch, Cory."

"Yes, ma'am." I wheeled around. Someone had thrown down a crumpled piece of paper. I punted it into the lockers.

The echo of Mrs. Irani's laughter followed me the rest of the way down the hall.

Follow the directions.

1. More tension builds if readers believe a character is unlikely to succeed. When Cory shakes his head, readers know it is unlikely that he will talk to his teacher about the class he wants. Put brackets around the passage that first shows what trait causes him to behave this way.

2. More tension builds if readers watch a character struggle to overcome his problems. With each failure, it seems more unlikely that the character will ever succeed. Underline the passages that show that Cory has failed in his attempt to talk to his teacher.

3. The most intense passages should occur when the main character makes a final struggle. What action or actions does Cory take in the moment of final struggle?

_____

4. When the story ends, do readers know whether Cory will be able to get into the class he wants? _____

When the story ends, can readers assume Cory has overcome his tendency to withdraw from conflict? _____

5. Is tension over at the end of the story? _____
How does the writer let you know? _____

_____

Believe It or Not

Newspapers provide up-to-date information about political developments, weather conditions, new scientific discoveries, and even local heroes. They serve as resources for students doing research, shoppers searching for bargains, and voters making decisions about candidates. Not everything you read in a newspaper is factual, though. Sometimes feature articles can contain opinions, and sometimes advertisements can contain facts. The following passages are taken from the *Houston Chronicle* during a one-week period of time. Read them and write F for fact or O for opinion.

_____ 1. Freed from the tight styling confines of its predecessors, the Cougar is cut like a gem.

_____ 2. At 8:30 a.m., an Egyptian jet, an Airbus A320, touched down on the tarmac.

_____ 3. The *Chronicle's* food section does not appear today.

_____ 4. Today's weather will be mostly sunny. High 79. Partly cloudy tonight. Low 57. Partly to mostly sunny and warm on Thanksgiving Day. High 77.

_____ 5. White and Home Sale Starts Today

_____ 6. These coupons can be used on a sale, clearance, or even a regular-priced purchase.

_____ 7. It's against the law to bring a loaded gun, fireworks, or flammable materials onto an airplane.

_____ 8. It wouldn't be Thanksgiving without football, turkey, and marching bands.

_____ 9. Fewer people are being killed by air bags.

_____ 10. Consumer advocates and government officials say the shift [in air-bag deaths] signals that a broad-based campaign for air-bag safety is saving lives.

_____ 11. 100 minutes. $19.95 a month.

_____ 12. The federal consumer safety agency has recalled almost 10 million playpens with rivets that can protrude, posing a strangulation risk.

_____ 13. A major new international study shows that school completion rates in other industrialized countries have surpassed those of the United States.

_____ 14. Kevin Smith . . . likely holds the key to the season-long mystery of just how far Dallas can go in the play-offs.

_____ 15. The Second Annual Landry's San Luis Official Galveston Island Holiday Lighting Spectacular! Friday Nov. 27, 5:30 p.m.-7:00 p.m.

_____ 16. Being No. 1 in total viewers is a brag any broadcaster would welcome.

_____ 17. Former Governor Ann Richards: one of the most dynamic speakers in the country

_____ 18. Dodge Ram 1500 Club Cab: SLT, V8, 43K, $17,880.

_____ 19. Marked vehicles assist motorists with minor automotive problems on designated Houston area freeways.

_____ 20. A pine forest was cleared for the parking lot of the Second Baptist Church.

_____ 21. Hurricane Mitch devastated much of Central America.

_____ 22. As part of a nationwide enforcement and awareness campaign for the Thanksgiving holiday week, a big effort is being made to ensure that motorists and their children are wearing their seat belts.

_____ 23. Dissatisfied with the financing details of the remaining two proposals on the table, port commissioners, at their monthly meeting Monday, called for a third time for bids to lease or buy the property.

_____ 24. The Internal Revenue Service is looking for 99,042 taxpayers whose refund checks never reached them.

_____ 25. We accept Visa, MasterCard, Discover Card, and American Express.

_____ 26. The best laser printer support in the business is here.

_____ 27. Unlimited weekends available for an additional $9.95 per month. See store for details.

_____ 28. Here's a deal that just might keep you from wasting your valuable time.

_____ 29. In addition to the daily price and change, other mutual fund information will appear on a rotating basis, according to the schedule below.

_____ 30. Easy to install and use!

_____ 31. These high interest rates available through December 11.

_____ 32. It is an impressive-looking facility.

_____ 33. After 15 months of mediation, Kennedy Heights residents and Chevron have halted negotiations over alleged contamination of the south Houston neighborhood.

_____ 34. Shop 8 a.m.–10 a.m. for additional discounts up to 30%!

_____ 35. No trash collection or recycling services by the City of Houston Thursday.

What Is It?

To test your ability to make inferences, play the "What Is It?" game below. First look at the drawing and the questions that follow. The questions help you to make inferences. If you cannot guess what the object is after answering the first set of questions, read the clues one by one and write your answers to the questions that follow each clue. Test how soon you can guess what the object is.

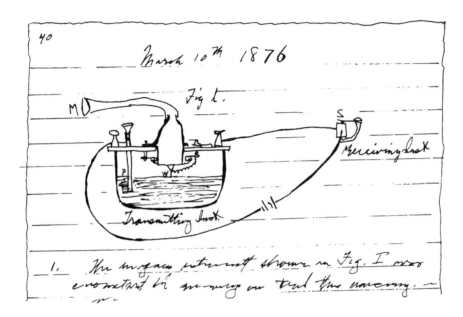

1. This drawing probably _____.
   a. is drawn using computer-aided design
   b. is drawn freehand

2. This drawing probably shows _____.
   a. a device that requires electricity
   b. an early type of water fountain

Clue 1: This drawing comes from a lab notebook dated March 10, 1876.

3. From that date alone, you can probably conclude that this device _____.
   a. has been in most American households more than 100 years
   b. may have been available to some Americans more than 100 years ago

Clue 2: This drawing has been on display in the Library of Congress's "American Treasures" collection.

4. This drawing probably depicts something _____.
   a. that is an important part of American culture
   b. that is soon to be developed

Clue 3: The mother and wife of the man who made this drawing were deaf.

5. This man was probably _____.
   a. deaf too
   b. interested in matters related to speech and hearing

Clue 4: This drawing comes from a lab notebook belonging to Alexander Graham Bell.

6. This drawing probably shows an early ___.
   a. telephone
   b. voice-activated computer

Watch That Attitude

Attitude with rhythm. That is what author Lisa Rowe Fraustino calls "voice" in fiction. Characters can have a voice, and writers can, too. Anyone who has read Roald Dahl or Dr. Seuss would immediately recognize another of their books, even if the author's name was scratched out. Word choices, the rhythm of the prose, and the attitude the writer adopts toward the characters are all part of a writer's voice.

Read the following passages. Notice the words being used, the rhythm of the sentences, and the attitude being revealed. Indicate whether you think the writer's voice is satirical, lyrical, scholarly, or punchy. Use only one choice for each selection, and do not use each choice more than once.

"It's okay, Mama," Kathryn whispered. "I'll stay with you." When her mother's eyes had closed, Kathryn kissed her on the forehead. She sat on the floor with her back against the mattress. Outside the window, the moon was rising, its edges sharp and clean against the black sky. Tears blurred Kathryn's vision, and the longer she stared, the more the moon's hard edges softened. When she drifted off to sleep, she could almost believe it was last summer, and Mama was still well.

1. The author's voice in this selection can be described as _____.

The rally fell short. Jersey Village trounced Cy-Falls, 24-3. In the final moments, left cornerback Matt Shiner threw on the run, only to have his final pass bounce off cornerback Kevin Young.

2. The author's voice in this selection can be described as _____.

Dixie Smith was a good girl. She went to school, at least some of the time. She helped at home, at least some of the time. And she only slapped her mother that once. Could she help it that she forgot she was holding a baseball bat when she swung her arm?

3. The author's voice in this selection can be described as _____.

The collection contains more than 363,000 measured drawings and large-format photographs. The collection chronicles achievements in architecture, engineering, and design over a period spanning three centuries.

4. The author's voice in this selection can be described as _____.

Name _____

☞ When you read an article, look for the source of the information. Some sources may not be reliable. Both of the following passages seem outlandish. One is a report of an actual incident and the other is a report of an urban legend. Read the passages, looking for the sources of the information, then answer the questions that follow.

Actual or Outlandish?

Pilot Bounces to a Landing—on a Power Line

Tukwila Fire Lieutenant Dave Ewing reported on a fun rescue last Thursday. While approaching Boeing Field, pilot Mike Warren's two-seater plane was tossed by the wake of a departing aircraft. He tried to regain control, but could not avoid the power lines. One wheel caught, flipping the plane upside down. It bounced on the power lines. When the bouncing slowed, Warren was left dangling upside down, 60 feet above the ground. Rescuers turned off the power before positioning two cranes beneath the plane. After attaching straps to stabilize the plane, they used a cherry picker to get close to Warren. They unstrapped him from his seat belt and brought him down. Warren should have felt right at home when being rescued. When he isn't flipping planes upside down, he works as a crane operator.

Man Breaks Leg in Fall from Roof

At last week's luncheon for women in banking, investment banker Cindy Barrett opened her talk with an account of an incident that happened to a friend's neighbor. When her friend's neighbor wanted to replace missing shingles on the back side of his roof, he worried about the roof's high pitch. He tied a rope to the bumper of his car, then secured it to his waist. He then climbed onto the roof, and over the ridge. Since he was working below the level of the ridge, the rope would catch him if he were to slip, he reasoned. Feeling secure, he had been working for about an hour when he heard his wife call out that she was going to the mall.

Before he could react, the car door slammed, the motor gunned, and he was jerked over the ridge and down the front side of the roof. He landed on the lawn at the front of the house. His leg was broken, but Barrett's friend reported that the man was lucky to be alive. Barrett said the incident illustrates the need to think through all possibilities before making a decision.

Write your answer.

1. Who is the source of the information in the article on the plane crashing into the power lines?

   _____

2. How did that person get the information about the event? _____

   _____

3. Who is the source of the information in the article about the man being pulled over the ridge of the roof? _____

4. How did that person get the information about the event? _____

   _____

5. In the passages about the two accidents, circle any specific details you find. Include names, dates, days of week, and times. You can include specific equipment, too, such as a *cherry picker*. Do not include general descriptions, such as a "car" or "about an hour."

6. Think about the sources of the information and about how much specific information you have about each accident. Which do you think is the urban legend? _____

7. Think of an event you have heard about but now suspect is an urban legend. Write down as many facts as you know about the event.

   To whom did it occur? _____

   Who witnessed it and reported it to you? _____

   When did it occur? _____

   What happened? _____

   Any other facts? _____

8. Think of an event you witnessed. Write down as many facts as you remember.

   To whom did it occur? _____

   When did it occur? _____

   What happened? _____

   Any other facts? _____

Tragedy Leads to New Safeguards

Ceary Johnson thought the world was ending. Burning debris rained from the sky. A tidal wave rolled him 100 feet. It was 9:12 a.m. on April 16, 1947, and the French ship S.S. *Grandcamp* had just exploded in Texas City.

Stevedores had been loading the *Grandcamp* when a fire broke out early that morning. Twenty-six volunteer firefighters sprayed water on the deck. Ethel Vincent spotted the plume of peach-colored smoke from her classroom. Mary Hunter watched from the drafting room of Monsanto Chemical Company. Ceary Johnson was not watching, though. He had headed to a nearby cafe when the *Grandcamp* exploded.

Johnson, Vincent, and Hunter survived. Almost 600 others did not. Hunter was injured, and so were 3,500 other people. All but one member of the volunteer fire department were killed. He was saved only because he was not on the ship that day. The Monsanto Chemical Company and many other businesses and homes were leveled. Many feared that an atomic bomb had hit their city. The blast was 300 times more powerful than the Oklahoma City bomb that would occur almost 50 years later.

The world did not end that day, as Ceary Johnson feared. Texas City might have ceased to exist, though. Refineries and docks were shattered. Falling debris started fires that went on for days. Funerals went on for weeks.

The citizens would not allow their town to die. Workers flooded in to help. Monsanto and other companies rebuilt.

Townspeople vowed to be better prepared for disasters. Companies pledged to help one another. New safety procedures were put into effect. Other port cities passed safety procedures, too. Because of a terrible tragedy, many lives may have been saved.

Write Cause or Effect for each pair of sentences:

_____ 1. Ceary Johnson thought the world was ending.

_____ 2. The S.S. *Grandcamp* exploded.

_____ 3. The Texas City explosion killed almost 600 people and destroyed many buildings.

_____ 4. Firefighters could not stop the fire on the S.S. *Grandcamp*.

_____ 5. A fire broke out on the S.S. *Grandcamp*.

_____ 6. Ethel Vincent spotted smoke from her classroom.

_____ 7. The Texas City explosion killed almost 600 people and destroyed many buildings.

_____ 8. Port cities passed new safety rules.

You Can Kill a Horse But Not a Cadillac

A large city wants its citizens to vote for a bond issue to pay for a new sports stadium. They need a catchy slogan. A good slogan might be short or humorous, have broad associations or snob appeal, or hint "I'm like you." It might appeal to sentiment, use alliteration or rhyme to make it easy to remember, or feature a well-liked person. This slogan must be something like a political slogan and something like a slogan for a product. What elements might be typical of both? Read the slogans used in real campaigns. Decide whether the slogan is political or commercial. List one or two elements used in each.

1. Cadillac's 1905 slogan "You Can Kill a Horse But Not a Cadillac"
   Circle: Political or Commercial
   List elements used: _____ _____

2. "I Like Ike" slogan used by Eisenhower
   Circle: Political or Commercial
   List elements used: _____ _____

3. Coca-Cola's 1948 "Where there's Coke, there's hospitality" slogan
   Circle: Political or Commercial
   List elements used: _____ _____

4. "Patriotism, Protection, and Prosperity" slogan used by William McKinley in 1896
   Circle: Political or Commercial
   List elements used: _____ _____

5. Kennedy's "Human Rights: Kennedy Cares, Kennedy Acts" slogan
   Circle: Political or Commercial
   List elements used: _____ _____

6. The "Striking Back" slogan used on a Russian commercial featuring a giant pack of Russian cigarettes hurtling toward New York City
   Circle: Political or Commercial
   List elements used: _____ _____

7. Johnson and Humphrey's "A Better Deal for Women" slogan
   Circle: Political or Commercial
   List elements used: _____ _____

Write your own slogan for the city.

_____

Name _____

Spying on the Spies

Someone has scrambled the selection that follows. Write 1, 2, 3, 4, and 5 to unscramble these paragraphs and put them in their correct order.

_____ a. Unmasking spies must be exciting work. Not so, says Meredith Gardner. He is a famous cryptanalyst known for decoding the names of spies active in the period following World War II. He mentions the misconceptions associated with his kind of work.

_____ b. That 1953 execution still troubles Gardner. The messages he had decoded referred to Ethel as having knowledge of her husband's activities, but they did not identify her as a spy. She and Julius left behind two young sons.

_____ c. Deciphering those names required logic, a gift for remembering bits of trivia, and a willingness to do a lot of tedious work. Although today's supercomputers could decode World War II and cold war-era messages with little trouble, those supercomputers were not available when Gardner first went to work for the Army Security Agency. In those days, men and women pored over work sheets for long hours. Gardner was fluent in five languages. The agency recruited him in 1941, soon after the Japanese attack on Pearl Harbor. Within three months, he had learned Japanese, too.

_____ d. Still, Gardner knows that the difficulty and tediousness of his work made an impact. Historians studying new releases of cold war documents point to the serious breaches in U.S. security made by Soviet spies during the period. Spies secured blueprints for the atomic bomb almost two weeks before the initial test, one document shows. Gardner did difficult work in a difficult period in U.S. history.

_____ e. Despite his facility with languages and his logical thinking, Gardner studied Soviet codes for three years before making his famous breakthrough. In December 1946 he decoded Soviet messages first sent in 1943. The codes had been particularly difficult to break. The Soviet cryptographers were using "one-time pads" that changed the code with each message. When the volume of messages grew too great, some codes were reused. Gardner and others were able to compare messages, enabling him to make crucial breakthroughs. The codes he deciphered indicated that a spy was operating within the U.S. War Department's general staff. Although Gardner's work fingered several spies, the name of that first spy has never been revealed. Cryptanalysts and others speculated on the identity of that spy, but not enough information was obtained to confirm the spy's identity. Gardner did decode a message that identified an agent with the code name Liberal. That agent's wife's name was listed as Ethel, and her age was given. This information and the investigation that followed led to the arrest and ultimate execution of Julius and Ethel Rosenberg.

Now that you have unscrambled the article, use logic to unscramble the following words. Logic should tell you that the words probably have something to do with codes or with Gardner's work. Looking for common prefixes and word endings can be a logical way to start deciphering words.

1. U S I R T E Y C

2. M D O C E N U T S

3. Y P S

4. O D E D E C

Surgery at Sea

Inside the *Wind of Change*, a 40-foot sloop, a Russian sailor sat in a pool of blood. He was alone, and he was 400 miles from the nearest land. He was going to die, he thought.

The sailor, 50-year-old Viktor Yazykov, was participating in the Around Alone yacht race. This 27,000-mile race began and ended in Charleston, South Carolina. The first leg of the voyage required Yazykov and the other participants to sail 7,500 miles to Cape Town on the tip of South Africa. When starting out two months earlier, he had bruised his elbow. The elbow had abscessed.

Medical help was available via a Comsat-C satellite network. Sailors were connected to Dr. Daniel Carlin of the New England Medical Center in Boston. Dr. Carlin had already founded a corporation that he hoped could deliver medical help to communities too isolated to have medical care. Yazykov's abscess would test the helpfulness of at-a-distance medical care.

There was a problem. Yazykov's computer was solar-powered. He could not take advantage of satellite communications when it was dark. Yazykov's limited English skills also made it difficult for him to communicate with Dr. Carlin.

Dr. Carlin knew that something had to be done. If Yazykov's abscess burst, he could die. Just before Yazykov's access to e-mail was cut off for the evening, Dr. Carlin e-mailed him the 13 steps needed to perform surgery on his own elbow. Night set, and Yazykov was alone. Without anesthesia, he performed the surgery. The surgery went well, but he could not stop the bleeding afterward. Desperate, he made a tourniquet to try to stem the flow of blood. He strapped his arm to an overhead rail. By the time he was next able to communicate with Dr. Carlin, he could not move the fingers of his right hand. Blood had pooled around him.

He had not confided that he had been taking large amounts of aspirin. Dr. Carlin advised him to cut down his arm immediately, and to apply direct pressure to the elbow. The bleeding stopped and feeling returned to Yazykov's fingers.

Dr. Carlin points to Yazykov's recovery as a sign of what might be accomplished with telemedicine. Yazykov was not thinking about the future of telemedicine. Undaunted by his experience, this former paratrooper and disaster worker at Chernobyl focused on the next leg of his voyage. Once again, he was ready to set out alone.

No distances are marked on the Around Alone race route shown below, and the different portions of the race are not numbered. Draw conclusions to answer the following questions.

1. The Charleston-to-Capetown route was the first leg of the Around Alone race. How many legs does the race have from beginning to end? _____

2. The Charleston-to-Capetown leg is the longest of the race. Which leg is the shortest?

   _____

3. The Charleston-to-Capetown leg is the first leg of the race. Which is the last leg of the race?

   _____

4. After healing from the surgery on his arm, Viktor Yazykov was ready to set sail on the next leg of the race. Which leg would that be? _____

5. Which is the third leg of the race? _____

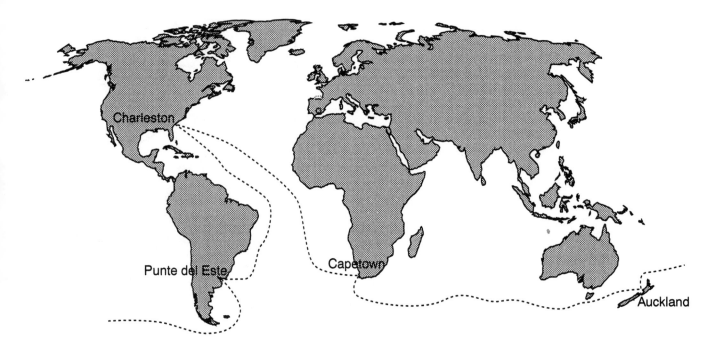

Boogie Over to Florida

A young advertising executive has just received his first big assignment. A railroad company needs a slogan. Its customers are tourists traveling to Florida's beaches. The young executive has to write a short, easy-to-remember slogan. It has to appeal to the railroad's customers. Perhaps he will find his job easier if he studies some of the railroad slogans from the past. Help him by circling the slogans that would appeal more to tourists than to freight shippers.

New York Central Railway's "Pacemaker Freight Service"

Union Pacific Railroad's "Be Specific—Ship Union Pacific"

Chicago Great Western Railroad's "The Corn Belt Route"

Northern Pacific Railroad's "The Yellowstone Park Line"

Ashley, Drew, and Northern Railroad's "Serving Southern Forests"

Florida East Coast Railway's "Speedway to America's Playground"

Union Pacific Railroad's "We Will Deliver"

Chesapeake and Ohio Railroad's "You'll Sleep Like a Kitten on C and O"

Saint Louis and Southwestern Railroad's "Blue Streak Fast Freight"

Saint Louis-San Francisco Railroad's "Ship It on the Frisco!"

Atchison, Topeka, and Santa Fe Railroad's "The Grand Canyon Line"

Utah Railway's "Utah Coal Route"

Long Island Railroad's "Route of the Dashing Commuter"

Saint Louis and Southwestern Railroad's "Cotton Belt Route"

Aberdeen and Rockfish Railroad's "The Route of Personal Service"

Reading Railroad's "America's Largest Anthracite Carrier"

Western Maryland Railroad's "The Fast Freight Line"

Now write a slogan that will appeal to tourists traveling to Florida's beaches.

_____

☞ Letters are a form of literature. Researchers often examine letters to gain insight into the lives of others. The information in a letter may not be complete. Sometimes researchers must draw conclusions. Read the following letter. Censors have blocked out some information that related to national security. Look for clues as to when the letter was written. What is the letter writer describing? Then answer the questions that follow.

A Letter Home

Dear Mom,

I would have written sooner, but we have been busy after ▮▮▮▮▮▮▮▮▮. If you have been able to go to the movies, you probably saw it on the Movietone newsreels.

Our LST ▮▮▮▮▮▮▮▮▮▮, but don't worry. I'm fine. The weather isn't making things easy, though. Yesterday, it was so ▮▮▮▮▮▮▮ that we ▮▮▮▮▮▮▮▮▮▮▮.

How was Thanksgiving? Did Uncle Aubrey have enough gas rations to come? Our cooks did a good job here. All day long, I was sniffing all those good smells coming from the galley. We had sausage dressing, though, and not your special cornbread dressing.

How is Imelda? Still getting those good grades? I can't believe that a year ago, the two of us were leaving the house together and walking the railroad tracks to high school. Tell her, if she sees Betty at school, to tell her Ray was thinking about her.

Ray

1. About how old would you guess Ray was when he wrote this letter? What evidence led you to draw that conclusion? _____

2. Was it likely that Ray's mother had a television in her home? _____ What evidence led you to draw that conclusion? _____

3. When was this letter likely to have been written? Circle the correct answer.
   During The Great Depression   During World War II   During the '60s

4. Why would the censors have blocked out information about the weather? _____

_____

Phone Research

Your world cultures teacher assigns a group project. Your group decides to do a project on Italy. Your mom works evenings at the airport, and your town is too big to allow you to bike everywhere, so you cannot offer to pick up supplies. You offer to do some of the telephone work instead. Using the table of contents shown on this page, answer the questions that follow.

COMMUNITY TELEPHONE DIRECTORY

TABLE OF CONTENTS

★ ADDED FEATURES★

Fold Out Map–Blue Business Pages
Spotlight Yellow Page Advertising–Green Section
Look for Our New "Kids Who Care" in the Green Pages

Write your answers.

1. You decide to find out how many Italian citizens live in your community. What section would you check first? _____

2. You find out that many Italian citizens live in your community. You also find out that Italian immigrants helped found your community. Since you hope to impress your teacher with your creative ideas, you decide to go to a city council meeting and propose an Italian-American Day, in honor of the contributions these immigrants made. Where would you check to find out when your city council meets? _____

3. You think *pizza* is a frequently used word that comes from the Italian language. You wonder if there are other frequently used words that come from the Italian language. You decide that a school that teaches foreign languages might be the best place to ask. Which color pages would you check first? _____

4. Thinking about pizza makes you hungry. After calling your mother and getting her permission, you decide to order pizza from the new place you heard about. It is not listed in the telephone book yet, since it is new, and you cannot remember the number to call for directory assistance. Where would you look to find the number for directory assistance? _____

_____

_____

_____

_____

5. Since your mom works evenings, and the city council meets in the evenings, she will not be able to take you and your friends to the city council meeting. Your classmate's mother agrees to take everyone, but only if you all meet at her house. What color pages would you check to see if a city bus takes you close to your friend's house? _____

_____

6. When you attend the city council meeting, Lena Gradnigo, one of the council members, meets with you afterwards and gives you wonderful tips. You want to write her a thank-you note. Look at the two residential page headings below; then write the page number on which you would find Lena Gradnigo's address. _____

120 Gordon-Gradney   121 Gradney-Grant

Whose Voice Is It, Anyway?

Characters have voices. Their dialogue shows readers something about their voices. Writers have voices, too, but their voices may be harder to hear. Word choices, the rhythm of the prose style, and the unstated attitude toward the characters can help you hear a writer's voice. Read the following selections; then answer the questions about the characters' and writer's voices.

Enrique stood with one foot on the ground, the other on the pedal of his orange Diamondback Sorrento. He tugged on the strap of his helmet. Then he swept his arm in a wide gesture that encompassed the meadow, the piney woods up ahead, and the narrow, sandy path that led into the trees. *"Difícil,"* he told Aaron. *"Muy difícil,* this trail."

Aaron gazed into the woods, his brows scrunched up. He scratched his head, then eyed Enrique's helmet. "That better mean easy," he said, "because this old clunker of my brother's won't handle the tough trails. I told you when we started out that I'd just look stupid if we tried anything other than beginner's trails."

Enrique grinned. "That's exactly what it means. Easy. This trail is very easy."

Write your answers.

1. Does the Spanish word *difícil* help give the flavor of Enrique's voice or the writer's voice?

   _____

2. Does the word *clunker* help give the flavor of Aaron's voice or the writer's voice?

   _____

3. Does the word *encompass* come from Enrique's voice, Aaron's voice, or the writer's voice?

   _____

4. The writer uses word choices to create different flavors for Enrique's voice and for Aaron's voice. What do you also notice about the pattern of their sentences? _____

   _____

5. One character's voice seems confessional and the other seems clipped, revealing little emotion. Which character's voice seems confessional? _____

Name _____

☞ Legal documents sometimes contain unfamiliar words. It is important to understand the terms. Context clues may help. Read the following warranty; then answer the questions about the words in bold type.

Warranty/Disclaimer

The WHATISIT Company hereby **represents** and **warrants** to Customer that the WHATISIT SUPER II product
1. Will work sometimes;
2. Will do something, but we don't know what;
3. Will be free from all **defects** for a period of ten days from the date of purchase;
4. Will not be fit for any intended purpose.

This warranty shall be **valid** for a period of 30 days from the date of purchase.
Product warranty **inquiries** should be **directed** to:

WHATISIT Company
Where Street
Someplace, Idaho

Circle the word that might be the best substitute for the word in bold type in the contract.

1. represents: states   stages

2. warrants: guarantees   licenses

3. defects: abandons   flaws

4. valid: convincing   enforceable

5. inquiries: investigations   questions

6. directed: addressed   pointed

☞ The words in bold type in the passage below have more than one meaning. Read the passage. The questions that follow ask you to choose the correct meaning for each word in bold print. Substitute each meaning into the passage. Choose the one that works best.

The Birdmen Are Coming

"If you should see a monstrous-sized, bat-like thing sailing far ahead, do not be scared into a conniption fit" cautions a passage in *The Weekly Corinthian* newspaper. The **passage** appeared in the December 8, 1910, edition. The monstrous-sized, bat-like thing it described was an airplane.

When pilots were called "birdmen" and airplanes named "heavier-than-air flying machines," some doubted that planes actually existed. Barnstorming troupes of aviators soon **introduced** the country to airplanes, thrilling viewers in the process.

The term *barnstorming* arose from the pilot's habit of **landing** behind barns. The tall structures **sheltered** the planes from the wind while on the ground. In the early days of aviation, few airports existed. Pilots circled fields, passing up the deep green ones. That deep color hinted that the soil might be too wet. When pilots found a likely field, they **registered** which way the cows were facing. Cows eat facing into the wind. When pilots saw the cows' tails, they knew they were heading the right direction.

Barnstormers might know about cows and fields, but they considered themselves a cut above land-dwellers who knew nothing about flying. "Colonel" Roscoe Turner was a **colorful** early aviator who flew a Curtiss J-N 4D—a Jenny, as they were known. He flim-flammed the people who watched his aerial shows. With smoke pots mounted on the tips of his wings, he climbed a few thousand feet. A dry cell battery touched off the smoke pots. Then Turner spiraled down, all the way to the ground—almost. Before making his climb, he picked out a hill, building, or a **stand** of woods that would **obscure** the last portion of his fall from the watching public. With everyone thinking he had crashed, he pulled out of his spin. He flew below the level of the treetops or behind the concealing houses and landed in another field. In an interview with K.W. Leish for the Oral History Research Office of Columbia University, Turner **recalled** how everyone would be searching for the downed plane. Meanwhile, Turner and his passenger **stole** back to the fairgrounds.

Today people still attend aerial shows, but they do not have to be warned not to have a conniption fit. If Turner were still performing, he might not be able to fool his public as he did in the early days of aviation. He might still thrill them, though, as his Jenny spiraled down toward the ground.

Circle the correct answer.
1. As used in the selection, **passage** means
    a. exit
    b. crossing
    c. journey
    d. quotation

2. As used in the selection, **introduced** means
    a. proposed
    b. familiarized
    c. submitted
    d. suggested

3. As used in the selection, **landing** means
    a. touching down
    b. a dock
    c. the level part of a staircase
    d. taking off

4. As used in the selection, **sheltered** means
    a. housed
    b. shielded
    c. concealed
    d. exposed

5. As used in the selection, **registered** means
    a. listed
    b. enlisted
    c. enrolled
    d. noticed

6. As used in the selection, **colorful** means
    a. bright
    b. brilliant
    c. distinctive or unique
    d. multicolored

7. As used in the selection, **stand** means
    a. a small retail business
    b. a raised platform
    c. holding a position
    d. plants grouped in a continuous area

8. As used in the selection, **obscure** means
    a. hide
    b. little-known
    c. baffling
    d. mysterious

9. As used in the selection, **recalled** means
    a. repealed
    b. remembered
    c. revoked
    d. summoned

10. As used in the selection, **stole** means
    a. embezzled
    b. swindled
    c. slipped
    d. cape

Staging Your First Job

You are the kind of person who thinks ahead. In a couple of years, you will want a first job. Your neighborhood has a Randalls store, and you have noticed that a lot of teens work there. Randalls offers a Peapod service, which allows customers to order their groceries on an Internet site. You are too embarrassed to talk to the manager face to face, so you contact their site. You ask which position would be best for someone seeking a first job. You receive this description:

The stager is the podster who prepares the customer's order for delivery after our personal shoppers have carefully selected products from the customer's computerized order. The stager makes certain that orders are properly packed in numbered bins and ready for our delivery drivers to load and deliver during the time slot requested by the customer.

At Peapod we always look for friendly, people-oriented individuals who have strong communication skills, possess a high level of attention to detail, and have the desire to provide superior service in a fast-paced environment. We offer excellent advancement opportunities with a rapidly expanding Internet grocery shopping and delivery business, consistent step raises, flexible scheduling, incentives and bonuses, fun work environment and friendly coworkers at locations that are easily accessible, credit union, dental insurance, 401 K savings plan, employee discount, and more.

Write your answers.

1. Randalls probably considers _____ the most important when hiring a stager.
   a. physical strength
   b. accuracy

2. Randalls probably wants stagers who are friendly and people-oriented because _____.
   a. they will be interacting with the customers
   b. they need to cooperate with the personal shoppers and the delivery drivers

3. Randalls mentions that they want people who can provide superior service in a fast-paced environment. Would some shifts require you to work more quickly than other shifts? _____.
   Why? _____

Mystery Origami Project

Reading instructions requires careful attention to details. Follow the instructions below to make your own origami project.

1. Start with a square of paper. Crease it along the diagonal.
2. Next make a kite shape: starting at one creased point, fold two outside edges in so that they line up along the diagonal crease. Fold the paper.
3. Turn the paper over.
4. Repeat Step 2, this time folding the long sides of the kite into the center.
5. Touch the sharp corner to the opposite corner, and press the paper flat.
6. Fold the tip of the sharp corner back down, about ¾ of an inch.
7. Fold the papers in half behind, keeping all the layers in place.
8. Gently pull the neck away from the body. Press the base of the neck flat.
9. Now gently ease the head out, and flatten it.
10. Open the wings slightly.

You're all finished! Circle the shape you have made.

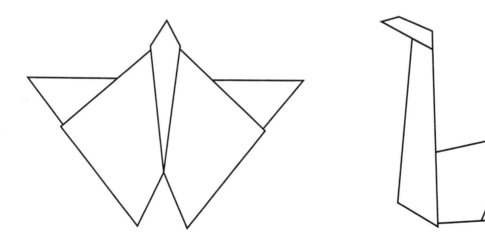

For other text-only origami projects, check http://www.rpmrecords.co.uk/bos/phone.html. For origami projects that include text and illustrations, check the site put together by The Children's Museum of Indianapolis. You can find an origami butterfly at their site at http:/www.childrensmuseum.org/bflyori.htm.

Select-a-Pet Exercise

Erika's mother has finally agreed to let her have a dog. Erika has fallen in love with several breeds. She wants to choose the cutest puppy. You tell her to choose a pet that fits her lifestyle. You sit Erika down and the two of you make up the following list about Erika's lifestyle.

1. Erika has an older sister who is in college, but no other siblings.
2. Erika has a cat.
3. Erika lives in an apartment in Florida, where temperatures are warm year-round.
4. Erika is athletic and runs two miles every afternoon after getting home from school.
5. Erika has lots of friends and they drop over often.
6. Erika's father is an at-home dad who has agreed to walk Erika's new puppy once or twice during the day, until Erika gets home from school and can take over the dog's care.

Help Erika choose a puppy by reading the following breed descriptions and comparing their temperaments with what you know about her lifestyle. Cross out any breeds that do not fit her lifestyle.

Newfoundland: These giant dogs are standoffish with strangers but loving toward family members. Their dense coats need frequent brushing and make them too hot in warm climates. These steady, intelligent dogs are good with children as long as they are raised with them. Not prone to bark, they can live in an apartment as long as they are exercised frequently. These dogs drool big time!

Greyhound: These dogs sport a short, smooth coat that requires little grooming. Ideal for apartment living, they can be couch potatoes, but also enjoy exercising outdoors as long as it is not too cold. Greyhounds will chase down small prey, so should be kept leashed when outdoors. Placid and gentle, these dogs can be socialized to live with cats and small pets if raised from puppyhood with them. They are not prone to bark.

Dachshund: These small dogs have smooth coats that require little grooming. Although active and lively, dachshunds live happily in an apartment if exercised regularly. They are prone to barking but like children and adapt easily to strangers. They can be difficult to train, so keep them on a leash when outside.

Miniature Pinscher: These compact dogs are between 10" and 12½" at the shoulders. Their small size makes them good apartment dogs, but special screens are needed on doors and windows. Their fearlessness, curiosity, and high energy make them escape artists. Sporting a smooth hard clean coat, these dogs need little grooming. They do not tolerate poking and prodding by young children, as their small size makes them easily injured.

Golden Retriever: Known for their eagerness to please their human owners, these dogs are easy to train. They love to stay close to their human owners but are just as friendly to strangers. They like other dogs and cats, too. They do not like being left alone, though, and can develop separation anxiety, leading them to destructive behavior. These dogs remain puppies for three years, and must have a dog-proofed environment. These active dogs do best with a big yard and a human owner willing to throw tennis balls for hours on end. Their beautiful feathery coats require brushing every day or two.

Dalmatians: These dogs are known for their energy and for their smooth, spotted coat. They require little grooming but do need lots of space and exercise. Males may reach 65 pounds. Extremely protective of family and territory, this dog can be aggressive toward children and other dogs. This clownish, intelligent, and "talkative" dog can be headstrong and requires basic obedience training.

Jack Russell Terrier: These small dogs are best described as feisty. Trained to go underground and bark at quarry to flush it, they consider any small animal their prey. Do not leave them alone with small pets or even with more than one other Jack Russell terrier, since they often challenge other dogs. Do not leave them alone with a child, either, as they will not tolerate even accidental poking and prodding from a child. These dogs are not recommended for households with children under six and, despite their small size, are not recommended for apartment living, either. They are barkers. The ideal dog for owners who value independence and fearlessness, these dogs require basic obedience training. Despite their drawbacks to inexperienced pet owners, these dogs are intelligent and entertaining.

Now that you have crossed out the dog breeds which will not fit Erika's lifestyle, you are still left with several breeds from which to choose. Erika has been thinking about other qualities she would like in a dog. She imagines a calm dog that will go along happily on her daily run. Since she will be responsible for the dog's grooming, she does not want a dog that will require daily brushing. Look again at the descriptions of the dogs not yet ruled out. Circle any descriptions that indicate that a certain breed will be calm, athletic, or easy to groom.

Which breed, from among the breeds she has not yet ruled out, has all three traits? _____

New Beginnings

Story and book openings must hook readers. They introduce the main character. They encourage readers to begin identifying with the main character. They show when and where the story will take place. They hint that the main character will be involved in some meaningful problem. This will be the main or external conflict the character faces. Most story or novel openings also hint that the character has some trait or fear which will make it difficult to overcome that meaningful problem. This will be the inner or internal conflict the character faces.

Read the following story openings. Identify the main character, the place and time where the story is taking place, and the character's main and inner conflicts. Then answer the questions that follow.

Story Opening 1:

Brenda stood before her full-length mirror. Elvis's "Blue Hawaii" played softly on the record player on the chest at the foot of her bed. She smoothed her pleated skirt and twisted to make sure her white blouse was tucked in evenly.

"Quit primping. You look perfect," her younger sister Susan said from the doorway. "Besides, you've given a hundred speeches before."

"But this isn't a speech. I'll have to answer questions, too. And I don't know what they'll ask." Brenda clasped her hands together. "I'm fine if I can memorize things, but I get so flustered if I don't think I know the answer. And all the girls are counting on me to convince the school board to let us wear slacks to school."

"Ha!" Susan said. Her lips twitched.

"Why are you laughing?" Brenda asked.

Susan pointed to the rolled-up jeans she was wearing, then nodded toward Brenda's skirt. "It's just that it's funny that you're the one who has to talk them into it," she said. "You never wear slacks."

1. Who is the main character in Story Opening 1? _____

Circle one.
2. The main character is about 10   16   25   45

3. This story takes place in about   1920   1960   1990

4. Which details tell you the time period? _____

_____

5. What room is Brenda in at the beginning of this selection? _____

6. Which details tell you this? _____

_____

7. What is Brenda's main problem or external conflict? _____

_____

8. Name two things that make this problem worse for Brenda than it would be for almost anyone
   else. _____

_____

Story Opening 2:

"Whoa!" Zack's swim coach said. "Don't jump in yet." He pointed to Zack's teammate on the Cy-Falls varsity swim team, who surfaced a few feet out from the edge of the pool. His dark hair was slicked back and he peered up at Zack and the coach. "Don't be in such a hurry," Zack's coach said, letting go of his arm. "You're going to get yourself in trouble some day."

Zack smiled, but as soon as his coach had turned away, he muttered, "Yeah, and I'll be in bigger trouble if I *don't* hurry. If I don't do well at this meet, I can kiss a college scholarship good-bye."

9. Who is the main character? _____

Circle one.
10. The main character is probably   high-school age   college age

11. This story probably takes place in   the 40s   the present   the twenty-second century

12. Few details were given about the time period. Most readers assume a story takes place in the present unless other clues tell them differently. Did that impact the decision you made about the time period of the story? _____

13. What is Zack's main problem or external conflict? _____

14. Name some trait of Zack's that might make it more difficult for him to get what he wants.

_____

_____

👉 Articles often have a three-part structure. They have a beginning, middle, and ending. In each section, the writer has a purpose for introducing material in a specific way. Read the beginning or opening portion of this article; then answer the questions that follow.

Skateboarding: Extreme—and Profitable

Anti-school. Anti-team. Extreme. Dangerous. These terms have been applied to skateboarding. There may be another term that ought to be applied—*profitable*. Manufacturers targeting those of you who are skateboarders turn a big profit. They capitalize on the popularity of American's sixth-largest participatory sport.

Write your answers.

1. What do you notice about the structure of the first four sentences in this passage?

   _____

2. What do you notice about the words being used in those first four sentences?

   _____

3. One purpose of an opening is to pull the readers into the article quickly. Look at the answers you gave in the first two questions. What two tactics does the writer use to pull readers into the article quickly? _____

   _____

4. An article opening lets readers know what the article will discuss. What would this article most likely be about?_____

5. Another purpose of the opening is to convince readers that this information might be interesting or useful to them. What method does the writer use to convince readers that this information might be important or interesting to teen readers? _____

   _____

6. In the middle of this article, you would expect to find more information about _____.
   a. how manufacturers promote the extreme image of skateboarding to increase their sales
   b. safety issues for teen skateboarders

Ka-Thump Goes Your Heart

Writers choose details that set the right mood for a story and give readers clues about what might happen. The following two passages take place in the same setting, but the writer emphasizes different details in each. Read the passages and the two story summaries. Decide which setting description goes with each story summary.

Passage 1:
Jon leaned a shoulder against the paneled wall. He breathed through his mouth, trying not to make a sound. Up ahead, the fire roared in the living room, sending long, sharp shadows flickering across the marble floors. It was dark in the corridor. Dark and cold. Jon shivered.

Then he heard the footsteps, soft against the marble floor. "Dad?" he whispered, creeping forward.

Passage 2:
Jon leaned a shoulder against the paneled wall. Someone had lit a roaring fire in the fireplace. He stared into the red and orange glow of the flames for a moment, letting the heat warm him. He breathed the cinnamon scent that meant his father had made his special spiced hot chocolate. He lifted his gaze to his father's portrait and noticed the broad shoulders that he shared with his father. He checked to make certain that his father's keys were on the table in the hallway. Then he called, "Dad!" and went running into the living room.

Write 1 or 2:

_____ a. In this imagined story, 16-year-old Jon Martin and his family have just moved to a new town. Jon has just completed his first day of work as a stocker in a local grocery store. While there, he met the manager for the Hurricanes, a local soccer team. The manager talked to him about joining the team, and Jon can't wait to tell his father.

_____ b. In this imagined story, Jon and his family have moved into a mansion built in 1897. Jon has been hearing noises for weeks, but no one believes him. A few moments earlier, he was studying in his room when he heard his father's hoarse cry and then silence.

Keeping Track

You take care of your golden retriever. Since she has epilepsy, you also keep track of her medications. You pay special attention to the details the veterinarian writes for you. You give her the medications twice a day, at 7:00 in the morning and 7:00 in the evening. When your dog develops a case of pancreatitis, a serious illness, more medications are added. Read all her prescriptions. Pay special attention to the details about the cautions and dosages. Then answer the questions that follow.

Phenobarbital 60 mg
Directions: Give 2 tablets twice a day.
Cautions: Do not stop giving the drug without consulting veterinarian. Veterinarian may supervise a gradual reduction in dosage. Stopping abruptly may cause seizures or lead to restlessness, trembling, and insomnia. Seek immediate medical advice in case of overdose.
Missed Dose: Give as soon as you remember for seizure control. If dog's next dose is due within 2 hours, do not give the missed dose. Then give the next dose as usual.

Centrine .2 mg
Directions: Give 2 tablets every 12 hours as needed for nausea.
Missed dose: Give as soon as you remember.

Metronidazole 250 mg
Directions: Give 3 tablets every 12 hours.
Cautions: Give the full course of this medicine. Even if symptoms go away, the infection may still be present. Symptoms may recur if treatment is stopped too soon.
Missed Dose: Give as soon as you remember. If your dog's next dose is due within 2 hours, give a single dose now and skip the rest.

Baytril No. 68
Directions: Administer 1½ tablets twice daily.
Cautions: Give the full course of this medication. Even if symptoms go away, infection may still be present. Symptoms may recur if treatment is stopped too soon.
Missed Dose: Give as soon as you remember.

Potassium Bromide Capsules 1000 mg
Directions: Give one capsule each day.
Cautions: Give with food. Do not discontinue this medication without consulting veterinarian. Stopping abruptly may lead to seizures.
Missed Dose: Give as soon as you remember.

Write the answer.

1. It is seven in the morning, and you are rushing to get to school. You have given your dog two Centrine tablets, two phenobarbital tablets, two metronidazole tablets, one and a half Baytril tablets, and one potassium bromide capsule. Is this all she needs before you leave for school?

    _____

    If not, what else does your dog need? _____

2. It is seven in the evening of that same day, and your dog no longer seems to have an upset stomach. You have given her two phenobarbital tablets, one and a half Baytril tablets, and three metronidazole tablets. Is this all she needs for this evening? _____

    If not, what else does your dog need? _____

3. Your dog does not show signs of an upset stomach all that next day. Which medications should you give her that evening, if you gave her the potassium bromide in the morning?

    _____

4. You oversleep the next morning and forget the dog's medicine. You remember when you get home from school at 3:00. Should you give your dog her phenobarbital now? _____

5. Two days later, you measure out your dog's pills at 7:00 in the morning. You give her one potassium bromide tablet, one and a half Baytril tablets, three phenobarbital tablets, and two metronidazole tablets. When you get to school, you try to remember if you have made a mistake. Have you? _____

    If so, what mistake have you made? _____

    If so, what should you do next? _____

Rafting Iguanas

Do iguanas get seasick? The answer to that question may never be known, but 15 iguanas that set out to sea on a raft may answer other questions for scientists.

The iguanas did not intend to go out to sea. They were hanging around in a tree on the island of Guadeloupe, their native home, when a hurricane hit. One month and 175 miles later, they landed on the island of Anguilla. Witnesses knew they were refugees, because these 15 iguanas were green, and Anguilla's iguanas are brown.

Scientists had long wondered how small animals got from one island to another. Land bridges might once have existed, providing island-to-island pathways for some animals. Land bridges did not exist between all islands populated by similar species, though. Some scientists suggested that some animals might have gotten swept into the sea on a mat of mangrove trees or other plant material.

Other scientists thought the idea improbable. Even if it were possible that the animals could survive, how would it ever be proved that had happened? The 15 refugee iguanas provide the proof that this theory is viable, says Ellen Censky of the Carnegie Museum of Natural History in Pittsburgh, Pennsylvania. Scientists marked the refugee iguanas so they could observe what happens to them on their new island home. One of the females has produced a nest of eggs. The green iguanas are settling in fine. Move over, brown iguanas. You've got new neighbors.

Write your answers.

1. On the hurricane tracking chart, locate the two islands mentioned in the selection. Put an X on them. These two islands are part of what chain of islands?_____

2. Traveling from Guadeloupe to Anguilla, the iguanas would have traveled which direction?

   _____

3. Draw a circle around Guadeloupe, with the radius of the circle being the distance between Guadeloupe and Anguilla. If the iguanas could survive on the raft for the distance it took to travel from Guadeloupe to Anguilla, and if you could assume that the iguanas could survive a trip of that distance in any direction, but only that distance, could they survive the trip to St. Lucia? Could they survive the trip to Grenada? _____

4. If the iguanas had been carried out to sea by Hurricane Hortense, which direction would they have traveled? _____

5. If they had been swept that direction, would they have made landfall before traveling outside the circle you drew with Guadeloupe at the center? _____

6. Two of the three hurricanes marked on the chart swept across the Leeward Islands in September of the year the green iguanas were spotted in Anguilla. One swept across the Leeward Islands the following September. That hurricane could not have carried iguanas to Anguilla that next year, because it traveled in the wrong direction. What are the names of the two hurricanes that might have carried the iguanas to Anguilla? _____

   _____

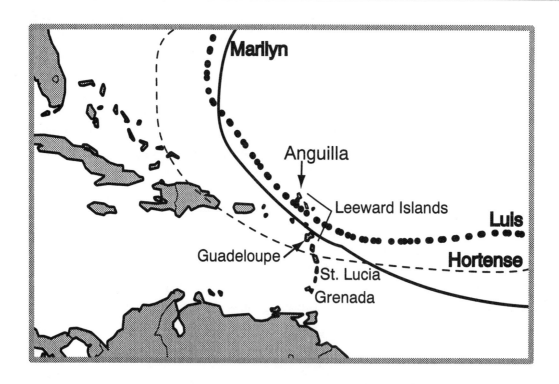

☞ In 1702 Daniel Defoe wrote an essay that landed him in jail. The essay was satirical. He pretended to share the prejudices of an intolerant group. By exaggerating, he made their prejudices seem silly. The following essay is also a satirical essay. The writer pretends to agree with a certain practice. Read it and look for clues that the essay is satirical.

A Better Use for Water

Every day, women traipse down rural African roads, carrying yellow 20-liter plastic cans on their backs. What is in the cans? Water. Water that could be put to better use. That water is needed to help large African cities grow. This paper proposes a radical solution to Africa's problems with water shortages—the creation of water markets. Rural areas would sell their water to cities.

Some might argue, how can rural areas sell their water when they have so little water for their own uses? That attitude is a short-sighted one. While some of the water carted into rural areas is used for drinking, washing, and cooking, much is used to irrigate marginal family farms. The loss of these farms, while of interest to the families involved, would not harm the economy of developing countries. A successful experiment in Arizona points to the benefits that might be expected. There, more than 50,000 acres of farmland were retired, and the water was diverted. Mile after mile of suburban development now stand as a monument to the forethought of those who took these actions.

Rural African farmers would gain more than they would lose. A few crops that are barely enough to sustain life anyway would be replaced by cash. What would be the result of such sales? To determine the answer, examples of similar transactions might be examined. For example, when Utah developers began buying water rights to be used in densely populated areas, the value of those water rights skyrocketed. Farmers in rural Africa might expect to see the prices for their water rights rise in a similar manner.

"What about the women and children who live on those small African farms?" short-sighted naysayers might cry. What will they do with money? Lots. For example, those women who are now forced to carry water on their backs could buy cars. With cars, they could drive to the cities. They could buy their water there.

Write three clues that the writer gives you that the essay is satirical:

1. _____

2. _____

3. _____

☞ The main idea of a passage tells what the passage is about. The main idea may be stated, but sometimes it is not. The main idea of the following passage is not stated. Read the passage and notice the details. Think about how they are related. Then answer the questions that follow.

Nit-Picking

A bird spread-eagles itself on top of an anthill. Is it undergoing some sort of ritualistic torture? Probably not. Ants secrete a substance that acts like an antibiotic. Birds do not. The bird may be seeking that substance to rub over its feathers. Birds have also been seen rubbing crushed ants through their feathers or smearing themselves with the juice from onions or limes if ants are not available.

This activity points to one purpose of grooming—to kill parasites. Dale Clayton, a biologist with the University of Utah, calls this a life-and-death activity. Feather lice can destroy a pigeon's insulating feathers, forcing the bird to use enormous amounts of energy just to keep warm. The pigeon's weight drops. It does not live as long.

When male swallows are infested with mites, their tails are shorter. Shorter tails mean fewer mates. When female swallows choose their partners, they seem to prefer mates with longer tails, zoologist Anders Pape Moller says. A clean male is an attractive male, according to some zoologists. That may explain why a male horned guan, a Central American bird somewhat like a turkey, takes dust baths whenever he spots a female he would like to court.

Grooming behaviors do not stop once a bird has found a mate. Parrots form lifelong partnerships, and they groom each other throughout their lives. Scientists in France believe that these kinds of grooming behaviors may be relaxing. When parrot pairs have been separated, they groom each other more often for a while after they are reunited again. Other scientists point out that this grooming might not always be meant so kindly. Parrots might be checking their mates for clues as to where they have been.

The next time you see birds grooming, look again. You may be witnessing a courtship ritual, a life-and-death struggle, a cuddling session between long-marrieds, or the beginnings of a divorce!

Write the answer.

1. What kind of substance does a bird seek when it rubs crushed ants through its feathers?

   _____

2. Feather lice kill pigeons by _____.

3. Write the main idea of this selection. _____

Coasting Along

Jordan dangled 100 feet above the ground, her eyes wide and her heart pounding. She hung there for a terrified moment, and then she was plummeting nearly ten stories toward the ground.

Jordan didn't die. She was riding the Serial Thriller, a looping coaster at Texas's Six Flags Amusement Park. A shoulder harness held her in place but allowed her legs to dangle. Before the 90-second ride was over, she would travel a half-mile track that included a sidewinder half-hook, a full 360-degree loop, corkscrew spirals, and a double spin.

The Serial Thriller is one of a new class of roller coasters shattering barriers that once seemed unbreakable. Coasters such as The Riddler's Revenge at Six Flags Magic Mountain in California stand riders up four abreast. Coasters hang riders from harnesses. Some use magnets so powerful that the coasters don't need a long first drop to build up speed.

The forerunners of roller coasters were invented 500 years ago. The first coasters were tame by today's standards. Fifteenth-century Russians perched on a chunk of ice and slid down a long wooden slide. Soft dirt or hay broke their fall. In the 1840s American ingenuity transformed a ramp to an abandoned coal mine pit into the first American coaster.

The beginning of the twentieth century brought the first real innovations in roller coasters. American John Miller introduced banked tracks. His inventions also included the safety devices that kept cars from rolling back while climbing a hill. The cars could climb, and the popularity of the roller coasters climbed, too. Then the Great Depression brought economic problems. Scrap wood and metal were needed during World War II. These two periods saw the closings of many parks and the dismantling of many coasters. Afterwards, the popularity of the coasters rebounded as more new developments made them even more exciting. The first looping coasters were introduced in 1975. Theme parks battled each other to have the tallest, the wildest, and the fastest rides. Coasters climbed more than 200 feet. Some catapulted their passengers at speeds of up to 100 miles an hour.

When Jordan brings her children to a theme park some day, who knows what the next generation of coasters might put them through!

The following questions ask you to draw conclusions based on what you have read in the selection. Circle T for true or F for false.

T F 1. Powerful magnets pull coasters up the tracks in some of today's coasters.

T F 2. Coasters were wildly popular even before American John Miller's innovations.

T F 3. Coasters climbed over 200 feet before World War II.

T F 4. During World War II, building supplies were diverted to wartime uses. This probably contributed to the closing of some theme parks.

T F 5. Coasters once needed a drop in order to build up the momentum needed to propel them up the next hill.

T F 6. Amusement parks did not exist before the Great Depression.

T F 7. During the Great Depression, many people could not afford to go to amusement parks.

T F 8. Most coasters today catapult their riders at speeds of more than 100 miles an hour.

T F 9. Since the forerunners of modern roller coasters were so tame by today's standards, it can be assumed that they were also much safer than today's coasters.

T F 10. American John Miller was responsible for the development of the harnesses that leave riders' feet dangling on the new generation of coasters.

T F 11. The Serial Thriller was designed by American John Miller.

T F 12. The Riddler's Revenge was designed by American John Miller.

T F 13. American John Miller was working on roller coaster designs near the beginning of the twentieth century.

T F 14. American John Miller began working on roller coaster designs before World War II.

☞ Five minutes before the test, you have just remembered that you have not yet read one of the passages. Don't worry. Reading titles, headings, and subheadings takes only a few moments. You can gather information about the main idea and about some details in this way. Without reading the passage, scan the title and headings, and then answer the questions that follow.

Tattoos: Art or Something Else?

Do tattoos indicate anti-social behavior?
Your mom went crazy when your older brother celebrated his eighteenth birthday by getting a tattoo. She mentioned hepatitis and worried what the neighbors would think. Dr. James F. Hooper, a psychiatrist with the Alabama Department of Mental Health and Mental Retardation, would go further. He studies the connection between tattoos and anti-social behavior. Tattoos on the hands or face might indicate a total rejection of society, he thinks.

Tattoos mean commitment.
Even Dr. Hooper might caution your mother that tattoos do not always indicate psychopathic behavior. Saying that tattoos mean commitment, he mentions that people often get tattooed at times of change in their lives, when they want to take charge of their lives. Your brother's tattoo could signify his wish to take charge of himself now that he considers himself an adult.

Tattoos in history: from Egypt to Asia to Europe
Historians point out that tattoos have been around for a long time. Egyptian tombs pictured tattooed people, showing that the practice dates back at least to 12,000 B.C. The practice spread to China and Japan and into Europe. The Catholic Church banned tattoos because of their association with superstition. Not until tattooed sailors returned from the South Pacific was the practice reintroduced to Europe.

Slave, criminal, or aristocrat: all wore tattoos.
The rich and powerful lined up for tattoos. Because the practice was expensive, a tattoo was considered an indication of wealth. Throughout the ages and across the cultures, tattoos have not always indicated wealth or privilege. Mark Gustafson, a classics professor at Calvin College, studies tattooing used as punishment. Other purposes included marking one's marital status or beautifying one's skin. A person skilled in a certain craft might advertise his skill by a tattoo. When tattoos became easier and cheaper after 1891, some displayed their tattooed bodies for fees.

Maybe it would be best not to point out that last possibility to your brother. Your mother might still be worrying about what the neighbors will think. A display of your brother's tattoos might be too much for her to take.

Draw a quick concept map in the box below, using only the information you see from the title and headings.

Write your answers.

1. What is the overall topic of the passage?_____

2. Where did tattoos probably originate? _____

3. Name some of the groups of people who were tattooed in history. _____

_____

4. What is one of the worries about modern people who get tattoos?_____

_____

Now read the passage and check your answers.

Name _____

Let's Talk About It

You and your friends are returning home from a scholastic bowl. Your sponsor takes you to MacDonald's. You have just unwrapped your burger when you hear a girl in the booth behind you say, "It was an accident that I saw the topic before they gave it to us."

"Why didn't you withdraw?" another teen asks.

"It was my only chance to place in anything," the first voice says, "and I just couldn't go home from the scholastic bowl without at least one ribbon. My mom would be so disappointed."

You haven't seen the speaker, but you already know something about her personality and about the pressures she feels. You can probably guess what she has done. Dialogue can reveal plot, details about the setting, and the traits and motivations of the characters. Read the following conversations; then answer the questions that follow.

Passage 1:
"And there were all these high school students in there, just staring at us," some guy says. He speaks with a strong emphasis on each consonant. "Some jerk says, 'I can't believe it. Some junior high kid is probably going to score higher than me.'"

"But how did you do on the test? Was it hard?" a soft female voice asks.

"Of course it was hard, Simone! It was the SAT." A chair creaks. "Why are you still sitting there? Didn't you see me getting up? It's time to go."

Passage 2:
"Just ask him," a soft voice whispers.

"I can't do that! What if he says no? I'd never be able to walk into the cafeteria again. I'd be doomed to eat my lunch in an empty classroom, hiding in corners whenever the APs walk the halls. I'd probably lose weight and people would think I was anorexic, and they'd start feeling sorry for me. And then I'd have to quit school."

"Oh, Erika, you're impossible!" the first voice says with a lilt.

Write your answers.
1. What is the name of the character who tends to exaggerate? _____

2. What is the name of the character who might tend to live through a friend's experiences and to be too passive a person? _____

Whose Viewpoint Is This?

Dear *The Eagle's Flight* editor,

On the announcements yesterday, Mrs. Pate said that all the school newspapers are staying in the bins. No one is reading them. She wanted to know why more of us aren't picking up our copies of the newspaper. I'll tell you why. I read the first two issues this school year. All the students interviewed in the "Eagle Talk" column and the "Tip of the Eagle's Wing" column were friends of the people on the newspaper staff. All the photos were people you know, too. My best friend Heather won the all-around title at a gymnastics meet, and you didn't even put her name in the newspaper, just because gymnastics isn't a school sport.

The Eagle's Flight is supposed to be for everyone at the school, not just for your friends. Put articles and pictures about the rest of us in the paper, and maybe we'll pick up our copies.

Write your answers.
1. This letter to the editor is not signed. What do you know about the writer from what is said in the letter? _____

   _____

2. In her view, is the newspaper one that represents all students? _____
   If not, why not? _____

   _____

3. Can you be certain that this student's complaints are valid? _____
   Why?_____

   _____

4. On a separate sheet of paper, write a letter to the editor of your school newspaper. Letters to the editor do not have to be letters of complaint. Be certain not to demean a particular student or member of the administration!

Croon a Tune

You're babysitting an eight-month-old baby. She is babbling, but she is not babbling words. She is babbling song. You smile, but you don't sing her song back to her. A few moments later, when she babbles "ma-ma-ma-ma," you do repeat the syllables back.

You may have made a mistake. Her developing language skills are being reinforced. Her musical ability is not. She is getting a strong message that her music is not as appreciated as her words. Her interest in music may wither.

Scientists have long known that children's language skills may never catch up if their first babbled words are ignored. Some say that the same phenomenon may happen if budding musical talent is not reinforced. Few professional violinists begin serious study later than age seven or eight, for example. A study at Beth Israel Deaconess Medical Center in Boston discovered that some classical musicians' brains were measurably larger than those of people who had not studied music. Gottfried Schlaug of Germany also found differences in the brains of people who began studying music early in life. Michael Phelps of UCLA found that when a trained musician listens to music, one area of the brain is most active. When a nonmusician listens, another area is most active.

That infant may be as driven to create and appreciate music as she is to understand language. Norman M. Weinberger, a psychobiologist who studies the link between behavior and biology, points out three signs that she may be responding to a biological cue. One sign is that all cultures have music. Also, a behavior with biological roots might show up in infancy. Your young charge's song might not have won her any awards at a talent contest, but research confirms that by 11 months of age, infants can distinguish melodies. They detect changes in rhythm. Some musical abilities do show up in infancy, then.

Recent advances in brain imaging point out a third evidence of the biological basis of music. Using PET scans, scientists study how the brain responds to music. Most language functions are controlled by an area in the left half of the brain. Listening to melodies—the part of a song we hum—produced brain activity in the same area. Other elements of musical interpretation turned out to be controlled by different areas of the brain.

Why should we care if an infant's budding musical talent is nourished? If it isn't, she may never realize her full musical ability. Society may lose a budding talent. She may also never be as good at math as she might have been. Researchers have discovered that young children involved in music training have increased spatial skills—skills used in mathematics. Weinberger points out that this advantage occurs only when music training begins early in life.

The next time you are babysitting and an infant croons a song to you, croon it right back to her. You may be helping to develop another classical musician or theoretical mathematician.

The writer of the passage on the previous page is attempting to persuade readers to take a certain action. The writer wants readers to recognize the importance of reinforcing an infant's budding interest in music. The supporting arguments include many comparisons of language abilities with musical abilities.

1. Based on what you read in the passage, name four ways language and music development are similar.

   _____

   _____

   _____

   _____

   _____

   _____

2. Name two ways language and music development are different.

   _____

   _____

   _____

   _____

Compare what happens in the brain when a trained musician listens to music to what happens when an untrained musician listens to music.

   _____

   _____

Beep, Beep

UR 2 good 2 be 4 gotten.

2 y y u r 2 y y u b
I c u r 2 y y 4 me.

Your parents might have written these coded messages in their friends' yearbooks, but your parents could never have imagined the extensive numerical codes needed to communicate via beepers. Even though the new beepers include word messages, Shaniqua and her best friend, Gabriela, still own the old style. All their friends recognize some of the codes, since they are common ones. Gabriela found more codes at the Sharp Communication Paging Codes Internet site. Now they combine the two codes to keep their messages private. Here is their message. On the next page, you will find a listing of the well-known beeper codes, as well as those at the Sharp Communication Paging Codes site. Use the two sets of codes to decode the following message. Each bit of code is separated from the previous one by an *.

Shaniqua:	121*411
Gabriela:	1177*87**401773
Shaniqua:	90*90*90*110*315*504
Gabriela:	209

Twenty minutes later:

Gabriela:	220
Shaniqua:	101*219*1177*87*401773
Gabriela:	209
Shaniqua:	90*90*90*101*202*318*112
Gabriela:	30
Shaniqua:	117*5012124*90*401773
Gabriela:	66*86*600
Shaniqua:	379919*58*1701*110*321*312
Gabriela:	707*54321
Shaniqua:	477*637

To decode the messages Shaniqua and Gabriela are sending each other, take a look at these codes.

Familiar beeper codes.

121	I need to talk to you alone.
1701	Live long and prosper.
30	This is getting old.
411	I need some information.
86	You're finished.
811	Not an emergency, but really important.
117*5012124	I'm sorry.
1177*87*401773	I'm at home.
90*90*90	No, no, no.
637	Always and forever.
477	Best friends.
707	Laugh out loud.
54321	I'm on my way.
379919	Giggle.
58	Happy B-day.
66	I'm mad.
101	Plans changed.
90*401773	Go home.

Some of the codes found at the Sharp Communication Paging Codes Site:

110	Go to.
112	Leaving.
202	Do not meet me.
209	On my way.
504	Fairly Urgent/A.S.A.P.
219	Transportation problem.
220	Where are you?
312	Home.
315	Library.
318	My place.
321	Party/Social activity.
600	Attitude adjustment needed.

Use this space to jot down the passages you decode.

Shaniqua:
Gabriela:
Shaniqua:
Gabriela:

Twenty minutes later:

Gabriela:
Shaniqua:
Gabriela:
Shaniqua:
Gabriela:
Shaniqua:
Gabriela:
Shaniqua:
Gabriela:
Shaniqua:

The Integration of Major League Baseball

Most people know that Jackie Robinson was the first African American to play on a major league baseball team. They "know" wrong. Moses Fleetwood "Fleet" Walker holds that honor. Walker was a catcher for the Toledo Blue Stockings, a team which joined the fledgling major league American Association in 1884.

The integration of major league baseball was short-lived. In July of 1887, the International League declared that no future contracts could be offered to African Americans. Not until Robinson signed with the Brooklyn Dodgers in 1945 would another African American be offered a contract with a major league team. Some club managers and coaches tried. In 1901 John McGraw, manager of the Baltimore Orioles, tried to sign African American second baseman Charlie Grant to his team. Renaming Grant "Chief Tokohoma," the manager tried to convince others that Grant was a Cherokee. Other managers insisted that talented African American players were Hispanic, although even Hispanic players were not guaranteed a good reception. In the 1920s Jose "Joe" Mendez was considered too dark to be offered a contract.

Some African American players continued to play on integrated amateur teams. Professionals formed their own leagues. They toured the country, playing one another and sometimes playing white teams. Some think that their success when playing against their white major league counterparts may have led to baseball commissioner Kennesaw Mountain Landis's ban of these games.

Although banned from major league play, African American players served as good ambassadors for the sport. Wherever they appeared, they drew crowds. In 1933 the first East-West All-Star game featuring African Americans attracted 20,000 spectators. A group of African American all stars traveled to Japan in 1927, seven years before Babe Ruth and Lou Gehrig visited there. They played to crowds in the then-new Miji Shrine Stadium in Tokyo. African American players toured Cuba, Puerto Rico, the Dominican Republic, and Mexico.

After 1945 when Robinson broke the color barrier that had been imposed back in 1887, the African American leagues faded away. Their legacy survives in the popularity of this American sport in Japan, Cuba, and other countries. It also survives in the renewed recognition of sports heroes such as "Fleet" Walker.

Place the appropriate events beside each date on the time line.

1884 1887   1901   1920 1927 1933 1945

Name _____

☞ Read the following passage. Does this writer's voice sound formal or informal? Underline sentences that use the words *you, us,* or *we.* Circle any slang words or phrases, and also circle any contractions. Then answer the questions that follow.

Creepy Robots

NASA Space Telerobotics Program maintains a "Cool Robot of the Week" site on the Internet. Some of the robots are cool, including the one that may take over your lawn-mowing chores and the one that lets you create your own works of art. Some are creepy, such as one that is described as "humaniform," the one that performs surgery on hips, and the six-legged walking robot from the University of Waterloo. The creepiest robots of all may be the "Army-Ant" Cooperative Lifting Robots being developed by Virginia Polytechnic Institute and State University.

For several semesters, student teams have been working under John S. Bay at the Bradley Department of Electrical Engineering to develop a team of "army-ant" robots. Bay's description of the planned robot project is chilling. A robot about the size of a toaster oven will sense a load to be lifted. It will scoot under the load and lift it onto its back. Meanwhile, it will be sending out "help" signals to other identical robots. They will swarm the load, also crawling underneath and lifting it. Working cooperatively, these robots will transport the load, lower it, and scoot out from underneath. With the load transported, they will go about their business. They may search for another load or else cruise around on "mere exploration," Bay says.

Is that creepy, or what? That isn't all. These robots will have heads mounted on little masts. Those heads will be able to turn 360 degrees. The scariest part of all about this robot system is that Bay expects to see something called "emergent group behavior." He points to the behavior of social insects such as ants. Behaviorists mention that ants and bees seem to have a group intelligence that advances beyond that of the individual animals.

Okay, so we know what Bay means. He doesn't mean that these colonies of "army-ant" robots are going to get together, decide on a scheme to take over the world, and then come after us humans. He just means that they will work together and that an individual robot might be sacrificed now and then for the good of the group, just as an individual ant might be sacrificed for the good of the colony. Still, the whole idea is creepy, isn't it?

Creepy. And maybe a little cool, too. If you would like to know more about how the project is proceeding, check it out at http://armyant.ee.vt.edu/paper/robo_mag.html.

1. Would you label this writer's voice formal or informal?_____

2. Would this article be best for a scholarly journal or a popular magazine? _____

Name _____

☞ The passage below includes words in bold type. Some of these words may be unfamiliar. To help you decide what a word means, look for a word you know inside each new word. The words inside will help you guess the meanings of the new words.

Candid Camera Kid Still Kids Around

Nerds, class clowns, goof-offs, troublemakers. They will never amount to anything. Or will they? You probably know someone like Howie Mandel, stand-up comic and host of his own talk show on UPN in the late '90s, but a bad boy in school. To find someone like him, look for the guy at the back of the room who has his best friend snorting laughter but who never says anything out loud.

At least that was what Mandel **proclaimed** in an interview with *Kidsday* staff reporters. Although he **recollects** always being good at making funny voices, he said he was shy and did not talk much in school. When he visited Roseanne Arnold's talk show, he painted a different portrait of his school days. He mentioned one **occurrence** brought about by his admiration of the television program *Candid Camera*. He decided to create his own episode. He dialed area **contractors,** told them that a new addition was planned for the school library, and invited them to place bids. When they showed up and began taking measurements, school officials wanted to know who had authorized them to bid for a new project. Howie Mandel had, they told school officials. Mandel soon found himself in the principal's office. His principal **disclosed** his actions to his parents. That incident and others led to Mandel's eventual **banishment** from school.

Mandel is not the only person who showed special abilities early in life but did not know how to turn those abilities to advantage until much later. While still in middle school, one movie **consultant** developed an obsession some might have considered nerdy—an interest in anything to do with the Civil War. One architecture student **recounts** how one of her high school teachers used to stand at the classroom door with her hand out. She was collecting that student's markers so the student could not color throughout the class.

If you have a Howie Mandel in your class, you might ask him if he has ever **envisioned** being a comedian. If a classmate is like the architectural student who got in trouble for drawing, maybe a career in architecture or art might be in store for her. If a nerdy classmate is obsessed with some off-the-wall subject, maybe you will **espy** his name in the movie credits some day.

Circle the correct meaning.
1. As used in this selection, **proclaimed** means _____.
    a. disclaimed
    b. announced
    c. demanded
    d. denied

2. As used in this selection, **recollects** means _____.
    a. gathers
    b. forgets
    c. remembers
    d. ignores

3. As used in this selection, **occurrence** means _____.
   a. electric moment
   b. current moment
   c. happening
   d. problem

4. As used in this selection, **contractors** means _____.
   a. lawyers
   b. attorneys
   c. builders under contract
   d. mathematicians

5. As used in this selection, **disclosed** means _____.
   a. revealed
   b. hid
   c. announced
   d. concealed

6. As used in this selection, **banishment** means _____.
   a. release
   b graduation
   c. escape
   d. expulsion

7. As used in this selection, **consultant** means _____.
   a. director
   b. advisor
   c. actor
   d. guide

8. As used in this selection, **recounts** means _____.
   a. gives an account of
   b. counts over again
   c. interprets
   d. complains about

9. As used in this selection, **envisioned** means _____.
   a. pretended
   b. made believe
   c. lied about
   d. imagined

10. As used in this selection, **espy** means _____.
    a. peek
    b. read
    c. notice
    d. ignore

66

Putting a Best Foot Forward

Amy Jong and Louis Marroquin are in the eighth grade. They want to apply to a respected high school in their city. Neither would write anything untrue, but both want to make a good first impression. Read the passages that tell about Amy and Louis. Make inferences about their personalities. Read the form that follows. Think about the questions asked. What kind of student does the school seem to want? Fill out the form for one of them. To persuade the school to accept Amy or Louis, accent those skills that you decide the school values.

Amy Jong

Amy's friends describe her as a take-charge kind of person. Her enemies describe her as bossy. She plays tennis competitively. She recently volunteered as a ball girl for a fund-raising tournament, meeting some of the nation's top-rated tennis players. She dreams of playing at Wimbledon some day. When a friend of hers could not afford private lessons, Amy taught her. Amy always shows up for their Friday-afternoon sessions. She has never missed a day of school, which might help explain her high B average. Tennis takes up a lot of her time, so she does not participate in other extra-curricular activities. Six months ago, she did ask student council members to start a campaign to collect funds for victims of a South American flood. The student council approved her idea. Amy was glad to let them handle the paperwork. She lectured classmates in her homeroom until their contributions were the highest in the school. After the pizza party they won, most of them forgave her.

Louis Marroquin

No one would describe Louis as bossy. He is the kind of guy who gets along with everyone. He would never do anything mean, but he disappears whenever there is a disagreement. He wants to be part of a group but does not want to stand out. During the campaign to help the flood victims, Louis's contributions were among the lowest in the school. He hated to badger his neighbors for contributions. Because of his high scores on standardized tests, he was identified by the Duke University Talent Search and took the SAT in seventh grade. He is a member of his school's basketball team, and team members appreciate the way he always works hard without trying to be the star. They voted him captain. He has been a Boy Scout since he was eight. One weekend a month, his troop helps repair the home of an elderly person, using donated supplies. Louis has attended more of these Saturday repair sessions than any other Scout in his troop. His secret dream is to be a politician, but he is afraid he could never make all those speeches. He has heard that the academy has a wonderful speech and debate program, though.

BRANEWORTH ACADEMY
Personal Inquiry
(To be filled out by the applicant.)

Name: _____School _____Present Grade_____

1. What do you enjoy doing in your spare time?_____

   _____

   _____

2. What community activities have you volunteered for this last year? _____

   _____

   _____

3. What extra-curricular activities did you take part in during your last two years in school?

   _____

   _____

4. What extra-curricular activities would you like to participate in while attending the academy?

   _____

   _____

5. Where do you think you would like to attend college? _____

6. What type of career are you considering? _____

   _____

7. Write a brief paragraph describing what you can offer the academy.

   _____

   _____

   _____

   _____

   _____

Choco-Raisin-Oatmeal Cookies

1 cup (2 sticks) margarine or butter
1 cup firmly packed brown sugar
½ cup granulated sugar
2 eggs
1 teaspoon vanilla
1½ cups all-purpose flour
1 teaspoon baking soda
1 teaspoon cinnamon
½ teaspoon salt
3 cups oats
1 10-oz. package raisins covered in semi-sweet chocolate
1 cup pecans, chopped coarsely

Preheat oven to 350°F. Combine flour, baking soda, cinnamon, and salt. Set aside. Cut sticks of butter into pieces. Blend butter, sugars, and vanilla until creamy. Add eggs, beating after each. Mix in flour mixture. Don't overbeat. Add oats, chocolate-covered raisins, and nuts. Mix well. Drop by rounded tablespoonfuls onto an ungreased cookie sheet. Bake 10 to 12 minutes or until golden brown. Cook shorter time for chewy cookies and longer for crisp cookies. Let stand for one minute, then remove to wire rack to cool completely. Makes about 4 dozen cookies.

If you prefer to bake cookies a few at a time, unbaked dough can be placed by tablespoonfuls on cookie sheet, covered with aluminum foil and frozen. Let cookies partially thaw while oven preheats, then bake for one minute longer than usual.

Write 1, 2, 3 for each step, putting them in the correct order according to the recipe.

_____ Add oats, chocolate-covered raisins, and nuts.

_____ Drop by rounded tablespoonfuls onto an ungreased cookie sheet.

_____ Preheat oven to 350° F.

Name _____

The Point of No Return

Why are writers so cruel? Everything goes wrong for their poor characters. The further into a story you read, the more that goes wrong. Then comes the single scene in which it seems impossible that the main character will ever overcome the almost-insolvable problems. It is the point of no return for the main character. That character must summon new strength or decide to give up. This scene is the climax scene.

Immediately after the climax scene, tension levels fall. The character has failed or has succeeded, and you know how the story or book will turn out. Stories and novels usually end with a brief wrap-up scene or chapter. That ending scene usually shows how the main character has changed. Read the following passages and circle "climax scene" or "ending."

1. Jaime surfaced. Already the scattered applause—if there had even been any—had died away. He climbed out of the water, wiped the water out of his eyes and tilted his head back to look up at the dive platform. Now he had only one more chance to qualify, and he would have to qualify with his worst dive.   Climax scene   Ending

2. "Hi," Michael said, sliding into the second chair of the trombone section. "Thanks for recommending me for team leader yesterday afternoon. I still can't believe you did it, after I was such a jerk to you."
Ramiro shrugged. "I knew it was tough, losing first chair after holding onto it so long. Your kind of competitiveness was just what we needed to lead our academic challenge team. But it doesn't belong here."
"I know," Michael said. He grinned. "At least not until the next challenge for first chair."
                         Climax scene   Ending

3. Tricia arched her back with her hands at her waist. That last aerial had hurt worse than the others. She glanced at her mom and saw that her mom's brows were bunched. She'd noticed. Tricia waved what she hoped was a jaunty wave. After what the doctor had told them today about that misshapen vertebra, her mother was already talking about pulling her out of gymnastics. If she showed any signs of being in pain, her mother would take her out in a flash.
"Tricia!" Coach David yelled. "That stunk! Put more energy into it."
Tricia nodded. But as she took off into her tumbling run, she could already feel the spasms starting in her back muscles.   Climax scene   Ending

Flavorful Speech

Comic Rosie O'Donnell often mimics the voices of friends and celebrities. O'Donnell's voice and her gestures convey the flavor of these people's voices. Writers use other tools to convey their characters' voices. Dialects, word choices, references to background information, and the rhythm of a character's speech can reveal gender, age, education, and outlook on life.

The passages on the left are excerpts from interviews or essays. Read these passages. The right-hand column includes descriptions of the people who granted the interviews or who wrote the essay. Place the letter of the speaker in the blank beside the correct excerpt or passage.

_____ 1. I aim to keep right on jest as long as I'm able. I'd a-heap rather do it than housework.

_____ 2. I knowed nobody dropped that for nuthin', so I didn't know if I should pick it up and tell them, or what, but my face burnt like a fire, for I knowed I was gettin' tested.

_____ 3. No one, however, could be expected to give a precise account of what did and did not happen in a moment of terror, and none of these inconsistencies seemed in themselves incontrovertible evidence of criminal intent.

_____ 4. Take the Washington Bridge, the Triboro Bridge. Plenty of men hurt on those jobs. Two men killed on the Hotel New York.

a. Seventy-two-year-old Mrs. Marie Haggerty was interviewed by Mrs. Emily Moore on February 20, 1939, as part of the Federal Writers' Project. Mrs. Haggerty worked as a maid.

b. Joan Didion is a celebrated essayist and critic of contemporary American life. The quoted material comes from her essay, "Some Dreamers of the Golden Dream."

c. Chris Thorston was 51 when Arnold Manoff interviewed him on January 31, 1938. This mill worker's interview was collected as part of the Federal Writers' Project.

d. Mill worker Alice Caudle was interviewed by Muriel L. Wolff on September 2, 1938. Her interview was also included in those collected during the Federal Writers' Project.

Write the answer.

1. What is the name of the person who spoke in short bursts? _____.

   Would you guess that this speaker was the kind of person who liked to chat?

   _____

   Would you guess that this speaker would have been the type of person who liked to discuss all aspects of a situation before making a decision or one who preferred action over talking?

   _____

2. What is the name of the person who felt her honesty was being tested?

   _____

   Would you say that this person tended to brush off insults or to brood over them long after they had occurred? _____

   If a writer were to base a character in a story or novel on this speaker, what kind of situation would be particularly hard for that character to face? _____

   _____

   _____.

3. Who is the person who intended to keep working as long as she could?

   _____

   Would you guess this person to have been someone who would rather have curled up in a chair on a Saturday afternoon, to read a book, or someone who would rather have been out somewhere? _____

   Writers sometimes use dialect to convey information about a character's educational level or place of origin. List two instances of dialect the writer recorded in this person's speech.

   _____

4. Which of the four speakers would you guess had the most formal education?

   _____

Accident Time

It is a Monday in April, but not just any Monday in April. It is the first school day after Daylight Savings Time begins again. You awaken to dark skies. Your body thinks it is the middle of the night. It is still dark when you head out of the house to wait for the school bus. You yawn all through school that day.

You are not alone, says Dr. Stanley Coren, a neuropsychologist from the University of British Columbia. Dr. Coren warns that people experience sleepiness for about five days after the changeover. Because clocks are set an hour forward in April, most people do not feel sleepy at their usual bedtimes. They may stay up later and then feel as if they are rising an hour earlier the next morning. Coren believes that this sleepiness leads to more traffic accidents. He studied 21,603 collisions occurring over a two-year period. He found that accident rates increased by eight percent the Monday after Daylight Savings Time began in April. When he studied the first Monday after Daylight Savings Time ended in October, when people feel as if they are sleeping in an extra hour, he found that accident rates dropped by eight percent.

Another researcher disputes Coren's conclusions. Alex Vincent of Transport Canada, the agency that watches over the government's transport, studied accident rates for ten years. He found a pattern in accident rates, too. Mondays saw an increase in accident rates, just as happened when Dr. Coren studied the accident patterns for those Mondays after Daylight Savings Time began. Vincent found this increase for all Mondays, though. He found that accident rates peaked on Fridays, dropped to their lowest weekend point on Sunday, then rose again on Mondays.

What about Dr. Coren's discovery that accident rates decreased the Mondays after Daylight Savings Time ended? Vincent did not find the same decrease in accidents.

Coren claims that other studies confirm his original conclusion. Studies of truck drivers and airplane pilots confirm that sleep deprivation does play a role in accidents, he says.

No one argues that sleep deprivation affects performance. It may be a while before further research settles the different conclusions of these two researchers relating to Daylight Savings Time. Maybe someday Coren's research or that of the researchers who follow him will convince school districts that students' performance is probably affected, too. Maybe it is time to campaign for a new holiday: The Sleep-in-the-Monday-after-Daylight-Savings-Time-begins holiday.

Write your answers about the sources of information in the article above.

1. Who is Dr. Stanley Coren? (Give his educational or work background to answer this question.)

   _____

2. Who is Alex Vincent? (Give his educational or work background to answer this question.)

   _____

3. Who is the source of the information that indicates that the fewest accidents occur on Sundays?

   _____

4. Who is the source of the information that indicates that accident rates dip 8% the Monday after Daylight Savings Time ends? _____

5. Who is the source of the information that indicates that accident rates rise each Monday?

   _____

6. Who is the source of the information that indicates that accident rates rise by 8% the first Monday after Daylight Savings Time begins in April? _____

7. Who is the source of the information that accident rates peaked on Fridays? _____

   _____

8. Who studied 21,603 collisions over a two-year period? _____

9. Who studied accident rates over a ten-year period? _____

10. Dr. Stanley Coren and Alex Vincent found similar accident patterns for one Monday and different ones for another Monday. Name the Monday for which they obtained differing results. _____

11. Suggest a reason the two researchers might have obtained different results for that Monday.

   _____

   _____

   _____.

☞ In this persuasive selection, some material is technical. To keep readers interested, the writer has used several techniques. The writer used contractions to create a conversational tone. The writer used the second-person "you" to make this material seem relevant and sometimes also used examples from a teen's life. The author also varied the lengths of the sentences to keep the rhythm of the prose interesting. Place parentheses around each contraction. Put brackets around any technique the writer used to relate the material directly to a teen reader. Circle any sentences of six words or less.

Take a Hike

Having a bad day? Did your friends make fun of your new shirt? Did your mother make an appointment for you with the dentist you hate? Did your first-period teacher give you a pop quiz? Maybe you ought to take a hike.

No, don't run away. Just get outside. A new science called *biophilia* suggests that humans have a built-in need to spend time outside. Blood pressure lowers. Breathing slows and deepens. The effect is so profound that some studies have shown that patients recover from surgery faster if they can look out their windows at nature views. That dentist you hate? Perhaps you ought to ask her to put a poster on her ceiling. Studies have shown that dental patients are calmer if they can gaze at a poster of a nature scene.

For a maximum calming effect, head for a park with green lawns and low, squat trees dotting the landscape. Across all cultures, people prefer grasslands dotted with trees. Scientists point out the similarities of this kind of landscape to the savannas where humans first lived before populating the rest of the world. Whenever we can, we've designed outside spaces such as these. Many of our parks look like savannas. Even in past ages, royalty often designed their play spaces with wide expanses of lawn shaded by low trees with wide-spread branches. They imported large animals to colonize these savanna-like areas. According to Professor Stephen R. Kellert of Yale School of Forestry and Environmental Studies, biophilia might also explain why attendance at zoos is higher than the total attendance at all professional football, baseball, and basketball games.

This theory has a flip side. If we have an inborn love of savannas, we might have inborn fears, too. Scientists call these *biophobias*. Some suspect that our fear of snakes may be a biophobia. That biophobia may contribute to our relative lack of concern over the dwindling rainforests, says Roger S. Ulrich, an environmental psychologist at Texas A&M University. Snakes lurk in rainforests.

When you take your hike, avoid places where snakes may lie in wait. They won't help your blood pressure.

A Lost Language

Manhattan. Rockaway. If you have ever spoken these words, you were speaking a language that is nearly lost. These words come from the Munsee Delaware language that was once spoken by the Delaware Indians of Long Island. Today only a handful of people are fluent in this language. Canadian linguist John O'Meara worries that the language may become extinct in the early part of the twenty-first century. Richard Snake, the youngest speaker fluent in Munsee Delaware, is in his early sixties.

O'Meara and Snake both hope something happens to preserve the Munsee Delaware language. Munsee Delaware is the only Algonquin language that survives. Delawares were Algonquin Indians.

With no specific program to preserve the language, O'Meara doubts that Snake and the others will be successful. When O'Meara first began studying Munsee Delaware, he made dozens of recordings of the speakers who remained. One day, listening to those recordings may be the only way to hear Munsee Delaware spoken.

This result was not inevitable. Another linguist—Thomas Jefferson—studied the Munsee Delaware language when the Delawares were still living in Ohio. The Munsee Delaware Indians had been driven westward by a 1640s war with Dutch settlers and by the settling of their territory. Many Delawares lived in eastern Ohio by the 1780s, when Jefferson visited them. He suggested that nearly all of what is now Ohio be turned into a reservation. His suggestion was ignored. Soon afterwards, a massacre of 90 Delaware drove the group out of Ohio. They fled into Michigan and then Canada.

Today, between 300-500 Delaware populate the reservation. Only about ten of those are fluent in the language of their ancestors. If you would like to hear one of the last of those speakers, check http://www.lihistory.com for a recording by Dianne Snake.

Read the passage below. Then circle the correct answer.

1. John O'Meara worries that his recordings may soon be the only way to listen to the Munsee Delaware language being spoken. He expects that _____.
   a. the few speakers fluent in Munsee Delaware will stop talking to outsiders
   b. the few speakers fluent in Munsee Delaware will die

2. Some place or street names in _____ probably reflect the influence of the Munsee Delaware language.
   a. John O'Meara's hometown
   b. Long Island

Discovery Rocks Scientific World

The light-colored speck glinted in the chocolate-brown sediment collected from the Pacific Ocean. The rock fragment was little bigger than a match head, but geochemist Frank T. Kyte knew he had found the evidence he had been seeking. He had just discovered the only surviving piece of the meteor that had slammed into the Earth 65 million years ago. The dark cloud of debris that blanketed the Earth as a result led to climate changes that may have caused the extinction of the dinosaurs and 70 percent of all the Earth life at the time.

The discovery of the fragment rocked the scientific world. Most scientists agreed that a six-mile-wide meteor had slammed into the Earth somewhere near the ancient Yucatan peninsula of Mexico. The Yucatan crater confirms the damage done from the hit. A worldwide layer of sediment from that period contains higher levels of iridium than are usually found on the Earth, pointing to more evidence of a past collision with a meteor.

Few scientists believed it possible that any fragments had survived the impact, though. Fewer of them would have expected to find the fragment in a sediment sampled thousands of miles from the meteor's impact site. Kyte found his fragment in deep ocean core samples taken northwest of Hawaii.

Brown University geologist Peter Schultz was elated to hear of Kyte's discovery. Schultz had already calculated that the meteor had come from the southeast and had hit at a 30-degree angle. The plume of debris that blasted into the air could have sent the meteorite hurtling toward Hawaii.

Some scientists disputed Kyte's conclusion. Knowing that the meteorite could have come from the meteor impact at the Yucatan did not prove that it did. Maybe the meteorite had not been blasted into the ocean by the force of that long-ago collision, but instead was a wind-blown fragment from another, smaller meteor hit.

Kyte points out that, although the meteorite is only about a tenth of an inch long, it is still far too heavy to be a bit of windblown sediment. He claims his discovery also settles another controversy surrounding the meteor. A meteor can be either an asteroid or a comet, and scientists had debated which the Yucatan meteor had been. The composition of the oxidized iron and nickel fragment proved that the meteorite was an asteroid, so the meteor is supposed to have been, too.

Many have worried that a similar catastrophe might occur in the future, and that this time, humans might be the life form that becomes extinct. The paths of comets are not easily predicted, but the paths of asteroids can usually be calculated far in advance. If that long-ago meteor hit had been from an asteroid, Kyte's discovery may prove to be more than exciting; it might prove reassuring.

Circle F(act) or O(pinion).

F   O   1. A meteor that slammed into the Earth 65 million years ago caused the extinction of the dinosaurs.

F   O   2. Frank T. Kyte discovered a fragment of the meteor that slammed into the Yucatan peninsula 65 million years ago.

F   O   3. Frank T. Kyte discovered a meteor fragment in deep ocean core samples northwest of Hawaii.

F   O   4. A match head is about a tenth of an inch long.

F   O   5. The meteor that hit the Yucatan peninsula 65 million years ago was traveling from the southeast.

F   O   6. The meteor that hit the Yucatan peninsula 65 million years ago hit at a 30-degree angle.

F   O   7. The sediment collected from the Pacific Ocean is a chocolate-brown color.

F   O   8. Meteors can be either asteroids or comets.

F   O   9. Worldwide, the sediment deposited 65 million years ago contains more iridium than is usually found on the Earth.

F   O 10. The meteorite Frank T. Kyte found was composed of oxidized iron and nickel.

F   O 11. The meteor that slammed into the Earth 65 million years ago was six miles wide.

F   O 12. Peter Schultz is a geologist associated with Brown University.

F   O 13. The meteor that slammed into the Yucatan peninsula 65 million years ago was an asteroid.

F   O 14. The meteorite that Frank T. Kyte found was a piece of an asteroid.

Solve the Mystery

Just before fifth period, someone scratched a car with a key in the visitors' parking lot. Two students claim to have witnessed the incident, and each casts suspicion on the other. When the officer on duty collects their class schedules, he decides that one of them is probably the culprit. Read their class schedules. Using the map of the building, locate their classes and compare their views with what they say they saw. Decide which one the officer suspects is the culprit.

Tammie's statement: I got to algebra class early. I didn't see it happen—the "keying," I mean—but I did see Matt—at least I think it was Matt—cut between the two cars that were parked there. At least I'm sure it was a dark-haired guy and he was wearing a red T-shirt.

Tammie's schedule:

Period	Class Description	Class Location
1	PHYSICAL SCIENCE	E103
2	ART III	C101
3	LANGUAGE ARTS	E234
4	US HISTORY	E203
5	ALGEBRA	E219
6	PHYS ED	B104
7	NEWSPAPER	E104

Matt's statement: She's lying. What kind of an identification is that? It's Spirit Day, and everyone is wearing red T-shirts. I think it was her. I was late to class and hurrying down through the library to get to the gym so the coach wouldn't kill me. She barrels into me right outside the library, mumbling something about how she was late to class, too. She looked worried, as if she was doing something wrong and worried she would get caught.

Matt's Schedule:

Period	Class Description	Class Location
1	US HISTORY	E218
2	SPEECH/DEBATE	D1O1
3	LANGUAGE ARTS	E234
4	PHYSICAL SCIENCE	E111
5	ATHLETICS	B101
6	ATHLETICS	B101
7	PRE-ALGEBRA	E228

Which student do you think the officer probably suspects? _____.

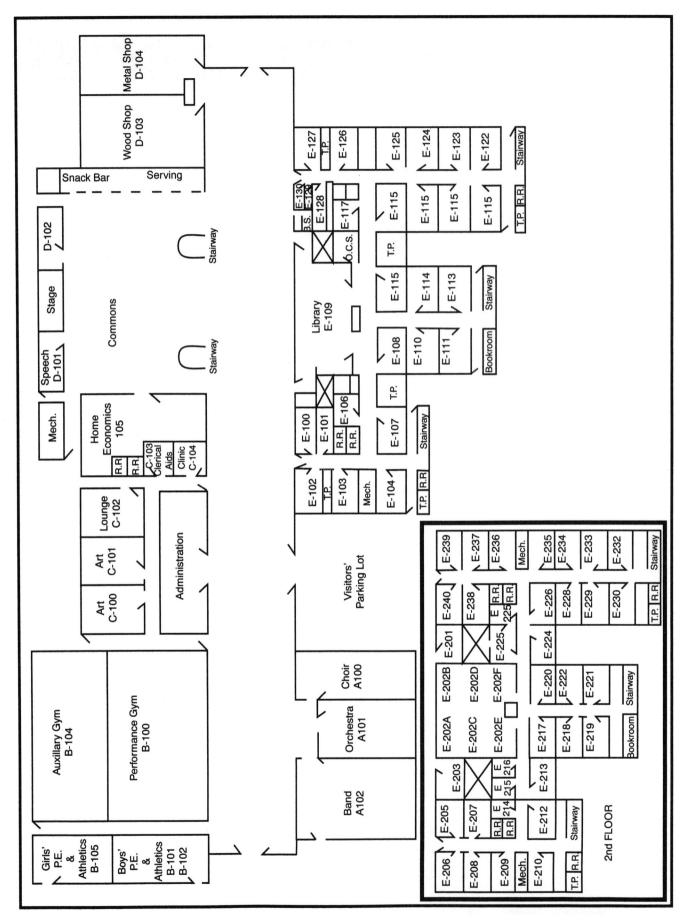

Conflicting Forces

You fly into the math class for tutorials, but you stop short. Your friend is sitting hunched over a desk. Her hands cover her face, and you hear sniffling noises. Your teacher faces the door. She puts a finger across her lips and shakes her head. You back out of the room, pulling the door closed behind you.

Because you care about your friend, you feel caught up in the situation. Is she having problems with a parent? Is she worried about her grade?

You feel involved. Writers use conflict to involve readers in stories and novels, too. Conflict can be of several types: conflict with another person, one's own abilities or traits, society or cultural expectations, or nature. Read each selection. Then indicate the type of conflict or conflicts revealed in that selection. Selections may have more than one type of conflict.

Caitlin glanced behind her, at her open bedroom door. "I can't talk," she whispered into the phone. "Mom is having a fit because I haven't started on my science fair project."

"Haven't started!" Mandy cried. "It's due Thursday."

Caitlin sighed. She glanced at her desk, where metal and wooden objects lay jumbled on its surface. "I know," she said, sinking down to sit on the edge of her bed. "I bought all the stuff I'll need weeks ago, but it just seemed so complicated and I . . . ."

"Did what you always do," Mandy said. "You gave up. Your mother is going to kill you if you fail another class."

1. Caitlin is the main character. What type or types of conflict does she face?

   _____

   _____

Patrick wedged his ankle against the ground and leaned back, stretching out his hamstring and calf muscles. "This cold weather sure is doing a number on my torn hamstring," he said.

Paul looked up at the sky. "Yeah, and it's supposed to get colder, too. What a day for a track meet."

2. Patrick is the main character. What type or types of conflict does he face?

   _____

   _____

Be Sassy!

Be sassy—as sassy as Sassy Nuñez, the sassy star seen every day on TFUN-TV's *We Are Cool* dance review. Sassy flaunts a new attitude every day, and so can you. Try a Sassy wig. Before you even tug one over your shaved head, you'll get to be sassy to all your friends, because you will be receiving a free 30-minute prepaid phonecard. Call them up!

Sassy wigs are for everyone—not just girls. But make sure that wig is on tight, because the moment you step into the hallway of your school, you're going to be caught up in a whirlwind. Everyone will be staring, and you'll be the center of attention! That new boy or girl in town who doesn't know you're alive? The editorship of your school newspaper? The starring spot on the cheerleading or football squad? They'll all be yours, because you'll be sassy!

Not just anyone can have a Sassy wig. We've made them in limited quantities. Call by 5:00 this afternoon or lose out!

This advertisement is obviously exaggerated, but it uses many of the ploys used in actual advertisements targeted to teens. Some of those ploys are setting a time limit, promising more popularity, mentioning a celebrity's name, and giving free gifts. Circle any of these ploys or other common tactics you find in this passage. Then write your answers to the following questions.

1. Are the promises realistic? _____ If this passage were an actual advertisement for a skin cream and not a wig, how would it make you feel about yourself if you were not the editor of the school newspaper or the star of the cheerleading or football squad? _____

   _____

2. Why do you think the advertiser would want you to feel that way? _____

   _____

☞ Political developments happen in a sequence. To understand reading selections that describe political or other developments, think about the sequence of events being described. Read the following passage about Lord Irvine of Lairg. Think about the sequence of events being described in this passage. Then answer the questions that follow.

Speaking Out

Our Speaker of the House ought to consider himself lucky. When he presides before the U.S. Congress, he wears a suit. Lord Irvine of Lairg was the Speaker of the House of Lords in Britain in the late '90s. He thought a suit beat his costume for comfort. He launched a campaign to be allowed to wear more comfortable clothes.

Lord Irvine was not asking to wear shorts and a T-shirt. What he wanted most was to be allowed to wear pants! His official outfit included a lace jabot and lacy undersleeves, slim black breeches or half-pants, black stockings, and buckled slippers that looked a bit like dancing shoes. He also wanted to dispose of the heavy, full-length wig and long robe he was required to wear.

His political party supported him. Not only would he be more comfortable, but also the change would symbolize the way they wanted to modernize the government. The Conservative Party opposed Lord Irvine's request. These men and women wanted to maintain the traditions of the House of Lords.

Lord Irvine understood the traditions. He had been named a life peer in 1987, and he took his title from the village where many of his forebears had lived. He had been a Queen's Counsel and had served in other positions which required a knowledge of traditions practiced in England's government.

A 145-115 vote allowed him the right to wear pants, socks, and regular shoes. All had to be black, and the shoes had to be well polished. He expressed his relief, even though the vote still required him to wear his wig and robe when he presided over the lords. Even better, though, would be the days when he met with the rest of his party members to discuss bills. Then he was allowed the privilege of wearing a regular business suit—just like our Speaker of the House.

Indicate the sequence of each pair of events by writing a 1 or a 2 in the proper blanks.

A. _____ Lord Irvine was named a life peer.
   _____ Lord Irvine became Speaker of the House of Lords.

B. _____ Lord Irvine was Queen's Counsel.
   _____ The official outfit of the Speaker of the House of Lords was determined to be slim black breeches or half-pants, black stockings, and buckled slippers.

C. _____ Lord Irvine became Speaker of the House of Lords.
   _____ The official outfit of the Speaker of the House of Lords was determined to be slim black breeches or half-pants, black stockings, and buckled slippers.

D. _____ Lord Irvine became Speaker of the House of Lords.
   _____ Lord Irvine was Queen's Counsel.

E. _____ A 145-115 vote changed the attire of the Speaker of the House of Lords.
   _____ Lord Irvine became Speaker of the House of Lords.

F. _____ Lord Irvine officiated over the House of Lords wearing black breeches, black stockings, and buckled slippers.
   _____ A 145-115 vote changed the attire of the Speaker of the House of Lords.

G. _____ Lord Irvine served as Queen's Counsel.
   _____ Lord Irvine officiated over the House of Lords wearing pants, socks, and regular shoes.

H. _____ Lord Irvine officiated over the House of Lords wearing pants, socks, and regular shoes.
   _____ Lord Irvine clashed with the Conservative Party over the clothing worn by the Speaker of the House of Lords.

I. _____ Lord Irvine's party decided on a policy of modernization.
   _____ Lord Irvine asked that he be allowed to wear regular pants.

J. _____ Lord Irvine became a life peer.
   _____ A 145-115 vote changed the attire of the Speaker of the House of Lords.

Texas Legend—Subject of Controversy

Texans are stomping in their boots! One of their heroes is being debunked, and they don't like it.

Since the battle of the Alamo in 1836, Texans have told the story of heroic defenders who fought to their death. They held off the massive army of Mexican General Santa Anna for six days. Sacrificing their own lives, these defenders provided enough time for the Texan forces to gather at San Jacinto. The vastly outnumbered Texan forces at San Jacinto were inspired by the cry "Remember the Alamo!" They surprised the better-equipped Mexican forces, winning Texas's independence from Mexico.

Davy Crockett was one of those heroes of the Alamo who sacrificed his life. Two young women survived the slaughter and told of Crockett's death early in the fighting. His body and that of slain Mexican troops lay just outside the chapel, these women reported. This gave rise to the legend that this hero had killed many enemy soldiers before falling.

A Tennessee frontiersman who had also served in the U.S. Congress, this colorful man had already become a hero to many Americans before he arrived in Texas. That he would help fight for their independence further endeared him to Texans.

Then the memoirs of a junior officer who had served with Santa Anna were discovered and translated. Jose Enrique de la Peña's story challenged the legend of how Crockett died. In his memoirs, de la Peña recounted how Crockett and six others had been captured at the end of the fighting. Santa Anna had ordered them shot, de la Peña reported. When Santa Anna's officers refused, others seeking his favor hacked the Alamo's defenders to death.

The memoirs were a forgery, cried some historians. An examination of the paper showed that it was manufactured in Portugal at about the time the battle was fought. Historians confirmed that the Mexican army was using that kind of paper, so that de la Peña would have had access to it. Although one historian still claims that the memoirs are a forgery, most concede that de la Peña did write the memoirs.

He was mistaken, some of those claim. Since the memoirs were written many years after the battle, when de la Peña was serving time for opposing the Mexican government, it was possible that his memories were not clear.

To others, Crockett's sacrifice remains as noble whether he died during the battle or afterwards, at the orders of Santa Anna. He sacrificed his life to fight a battle that was not his, earning the title of "hero."

Below is a portion of a military map that was drawn by a Mexican army engineer. The Alamo was not a single building, but instead was a walled compound that included barracks, a chapel, and other buildings. Study the map and answer the questions that follow.

1. The women who survived the battle at the Alamo told of seeing Crockett's body lying just outside the chapel. Draw a circle around the chapel.

Write the answers.

2. Sources say that the north wall of the Alamo compound was crumbling at the time of the battle and that it had been propped up from the outside with timbers. Santa Anna's forces could climb the timbers, and the final assault of the Mexican forces was concentrated in this area. How long was that north wall? _____

3. The northwest and southwest corners of the compound were filled in, creating ramps that enabled the cannons to shoot over the walls. Put X's on the northwest and southwest corners of the compound.

4. A peach orchard stood to the east of the compound. Draw a circle around the marks that indicate where the orchard stood.

5. What was the length of the longest wall of the compound? _____

6. The hospital was located at the southern end of the barracks. Put a cross—the universal symbol of a hospital—over the hospital.

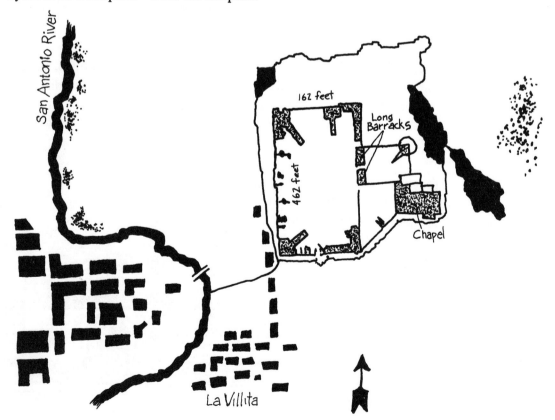

86

Tell the Truth

Angela leans over and whispers, "Dylan is in big trouble. He's the one who called 911 from the school yesterday."

Gisela rolls her eyes. Angela is always making things up. Nobody believes a word she says.

Angela is not a trustworthy narrator. In fiction, too, a narrator can be untrustworthy. Read the following selections. Decide whether the narrator is trustworthy.

Selection 1:
I sighed and said, "Sorry, but no can do. I'm grounded."
Carlos grinned. "What'd you do this time, Josh?"
"Nothing," I said. "Dad thinks I took the Wrangler for a joy ride." I took Ginny's hand and smiled down at her.
"So did you?" Carlos asked as the three of us started down the hall toward the exit.
"Of course not," I said, squeezing Ginny's hand. "I'm only 14. I don't even know how to drive."

1. Who is the narrator of this passage? _____

2. Can readers trust what this narrator says? _____

3. What clue or clues did the author give you? _____

   _____

Selection 2:
I sat forward, the phone cradled against my ear. "Try not to sweat it right now," I told Shawnte. "I told you I'd come over and help you study as soon as Mom gets home. When Jonathan Morris makes a promise, he keeps it. But I can't leave Hannah alone."

The drapes were open and I could see Hannah outside playing with our poodle, Josey. Josey hobbled after the ball. I got up to make a note to remind Mother to make an appointment to take her to the vet. The vet had told us to watch for any stiffness.

4. Who is the narrator of this passage? _____

5. Can readers trust what this narrator says? _____

6. What clues did the author give you? _____

   _____

   _____

Ask the Experts

Mona Lisa's face is dirty. Anyone who has gone without a thorough face washing for 500 years or so would have a dirty face. Experts have touched up age spots on Leonardo da Vinci's painting. They have layered varnish, resin, and lacquer on the 30-inch-by-21-inch painting, but they have not given the *Mona Lisa* a thorough washing. Now the varnish has yellowed her skin.

Taking advantage of computer imaging, the French art magazine *Journal des Arts* showed art lovers how the painting might look when cleaned. *Mona Lisa*'s cheeks would be rosy. The skies behind her would be a pale blue instead of the glowing sunset colors viewers see now.

Any attempts to clean Mona Lisa's face will be met with controversy. The Louvre Museum's top attraction, the *Mona Lisa* attracts 5.2 million viewers each year. Everyone wants this adoring public to see the *Mona Lisa* at her best, but they disagree on what is her best. Some experts, such as British art expert Alastair Laing, support the move to clean her face. Others believe she would look garish sporting such bright colors. Still others, such as Pierre Rosenberg and Jean-Pierre Cuzin, the last two chief curators of paintings at the Louvre, oppose cleaning the *Mona Lisa* for a different reason. Da Vinci developed the complex techniques used on the oil-on-wood work. Chemicals might mar its luster, these experts fear. Besides, *Mona Lisa*'s face is not as dirty as people think, Cuzin claims. He plans to use special lighting and nonreflective glass to brighten the painting.

Special lighting. If Mona Lisa had a vote, she would probably prefer to get all that stuff off her face.

Imagine that Cuzin and Laing are scheduled to visit your classroom. After the visit, you will be asked to write a paper comparing and contrasting their ideas about the cleaning of the *Mona Lisa*. All questions must be submitted beforehand in writing. Based on what you know of their positions from the above selection, write three questions you would ask each.

Cuzin

1. _____
2. _____
3. _____

Laing

1. _____
2. _____
3. _____

Silent Calls

Katy Payne was sitting on an airplane when it hit her. The throbbing sensations she was feeling through the skin of the airplane reminded her of something. She had felt this same throbbing while observing elephants at the zoo in Portland, Oregon. Were the elephants responsible? Some sounds below the threshold of human hearing could make the air throb that way. Were elephants communicating with one another with a sound below the threshold of human hearing?

It was easy enough to find out. Payne and her associates returned to the zoo. They recorded the elephants during the time they could sense the throbbing in the air. Then they played the tapes back at higher-than-normal speeds. What they found sent them to Kenya, Zimbabwe, and Namibia. The elephants had an extensive language humans had never heard.

Their sounds were infrasonic—below the threshold of human hearing. Humans cannot hear sounds below 20 Hertz or 20 cycles per second. The elephant calls were between 15 and 35 Hertz. Sometimes humans could hear faint sounds at the upper end of these elephant calls but could not hear the sounds at the lower end of the range.

The discovery of these sounds explained some puzzling behaviors. Elephants live in families of about 6 to 12 animals led by a dominant female. Sometimes one family associates with another family. Over long periods of time, the two families travel parallel to each other or move in big spirals. Miles separate the two families. How do they coordinate their movements? How does a family of elephants simultaneously decide to move on without making any sounds humans can hear? Once males reach adolescence, they range away from the family. Yet when a female is feeling romantic, males come from miles away. How does the female signal them?

The infrasonic sounds were responsible, scientists found. Payne's group discovered that the lower the frequency of the sound, the farther it carried. Dr. Bill Langbauer of the Pittsburgh Zoo, another researcher studying these infrasonic sounds, pointed out that grasses and shrubs absorb the higher frequencies of elephant sound but do not affect the lower frequencies. Payne's group verified that the elephants could hear one another over distances of more than two miles. They speculate that elephants may be able to hear over ranges of 300 square kilometers.

This infrasonic communication may also be responsible for another behavior seen in elephants. Payne and others have observed them freezing in position, their ears raised and stiffened. She has observed a hundred elephants all standing in this frozen position, in what she calls the "communal listening" of elephants.

Maybe humans cannot hear the infrasonic communication of elephants, but that does not mean we cannot learn something from them. Maybe we can adopt their habit of intense communal listening, so that we can hear one another.

Since Dr. Bill Langbauer pointed out that grasses and shrubs absorbed the higher frequencies of elephant sound but did not affect the lower frequencies, it might be useful to look at graphs that show which frequencies of sound travel most rapidly and which are absorbed most quickly. Below are two graphs. Study them and then answer the questions that follow.

1. Which graph would tell you that the higher the frequency of the sound, the more easily it is absorbed as it travels over a specified distance? _____

2. The infrasonic calls of elephants are between 15 and 35 Hertz. The middle point of these two frequencies is 25 Hertz. Put an X on Graph A at the point that represents 25 Hertz. What is the approximate absorption rate of sound at that frequency? _____

3. If Langbauer and Payne had been studying how quickly elephant sounds travel rather than how far they travel, which graph would be most helpful to them? _____

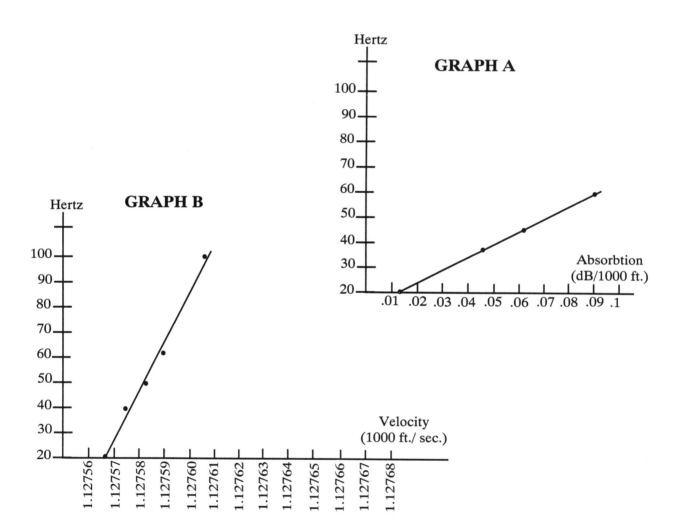

Name _____

☞ Sometimes a writer leaves some ideas to your imagination. Sometimes you can make inferences about what is not stated in a passage. Read the following passage and answer the questions that follow.

High Jumps: High Dreams

If Alice Coachman were growing up today, her parents might enroll her in gymnastics. As a child, she skipped, ran, and jumped through the back streets of rural Albany, Georgia. Even if gymnastics classes had been offered, she probably would not have dreamed of asking to be enrolled. Children growing up in the '30s knew that their parents struggled to buy food and shelter. Piano, dance, and similar classes were luxuries for the rich.

Coachman might not have dreamed that she would win 31 national track-and-field titles, either, but she did. She collected them on her way to being the first African American woman to win an Olympic gold medal.

Coachman's competitive spirit showed up early. She often challenged neighborhood boys to race her. Her tomboyishness earned her spankings. It eventually earned her something better—a spot on Tuskegee University's track-and-field team. She collected her first medal for high jump there, going on to win many more in her career.

World War II may have robbed her of her greatest victories. Not until the first postwar Olympics in London in 1948 did she have an opportunity to compete in the Olympics. By then, years of running and jumping had taken their toll, and she could not qualify for many events. At 25, she was nearing the end of her competing years. She considered not going, but eventually boarded the ship for the seven-day voyage to London.

That decision earned her a place in history as the first African American woman to medal in the Olympics. Her 5'6¼" high jump set a record that stood until 1956. She was honored by King George VI of England and later by U.S. President Harry Truman. Along a 175-mile motorcade from Atlanta to Albany, she was cheered.

When the motorcade arrived at the Albany Municipal Auditorium to honor her, she realized she still had work to do. African Americans were lined up on the left, and whites were lined up on the right.

The little girl who skipped, ran, and jumped the back roads of Albany might not have dreamed of all she would accomplish. Coachman wanted to make certain that other young African American athletes could dream of doing great things. She founded the Alice Coachman Track-and-Field Foundation, a foundation that helps young athletes realize their dreams.

Write your answers.

1. When the author states that children growing up in the '30s knew that parents struggled to pay for food and shelter, you can make inferences about when Alice Coachman was growing up and what her family's financial circumstances were. What are those inferences?

   _____

   _____

2. When the author states that Coachman's tomboyishness earned her spankings, what inferences can you make about the culture in which she grew up? _____

   _____

3. The author states that World War II might have robbed Coachman of her chance to win more medals and that she did not have a chance to participate until after the war. What inference can you make that explains why she could not participate during the war?

   _____

   _____

4. The author states that at 25 Coachman was nearing the end of her competing years and that she did not qualify for many events in the Olympics. What inferences can you make about her abilities at 25 and her abilities during the World War II years? _____

   _____

5. When the author states that African Americans and whites were lined up on different sides of the Albany Municipal Auditorium, what inferences can you make about segregation or integration during this period? _____

   _____

6. Based on what you read in the article, do you have enough information to make the same inference for all cities during this period of time? _____

7. The author states that Coachman's family might not have had enough money to sign her up for gymnastics classes, if they had been available. Is the author stating that money would have been the only reason Coachman would not have been allowed to attend those classes? _____. If not, what other inferences might you make, based on what you read in the article?

   _____

   _____

It's a Wash

The good news is, your allowance is going up. The bad news is, this increase comes with a new responsibility. From now on, you have to do your own laundry. You are good at mechanical things, so you figure out how to work the machine with no problems. When your white pullover turns out pink, you decide that there is more to doing laundry than operating the machine. Here are some tips:

- Read label to see if item is washable or must be dry-cleaned and to determine the correct water temperature to use.
- Check all pockets.
- Remove belts, ribbons, or pins.
- Shake loose dirt from the item.
- Treat stains before washing.
- Turn T-shirts with decals inside out.
- Separate items:
    light-colored clothes from dark-colored ones
    towels from clothing that might collect lint
    muddy or heavily soiled clothes from lightly soiled ones.

You are still learning. Over the next few weeks, you experience the following problems. What might you have done wrong in each case? There may be more than one answer.

1. Your white tank top has a wavy blue stain across the front.

   _____

2. Your khakis have white fuzz all over them.

   _____

3. Your white cotton shirt is torn at the shoulder, and your National Honor Society pin is missing.

   _____

4. Your new rayon shirt is shriveled.

   _____

Don't Scream

"Pay attention. Don't scream," the movie villain warns. Movie-goers tense. His short sentences call attention to what he is saying and create tension.

Writers create special effects like these, too. Short sentences draw attention. Words with hard consonants seem harsher than words with soft vowels. Words or sentences which have a one-two rhythm might remind readers of a heartbeat. Writers might use a single-sentence paragraph to focus attention on the sentence. Sentences at the beginning and end of paragraphs draw more attention than sentences in the middle of paragraphs. For this reason, writers sometimes bury clues in the middle of paragraphs where they will be noticed but will not draw too much attention.

Read the following passage. Notice how the writer uses the prose structure to create special effects. Then answer the questions below.

Kaitlin jogged, her breathing easy and regular. Early-morning sunlight slanted down, dappling the dirt path through the trees. The scent of pine was strong.

She smiled. Her smile barely changed when she heard a branch snap, and then another. Nothing to worry about, she thought.

Until she glanced back over her shoulder.

Run, she told herself. But she could only stare at the bearded figure approaching her at a lope. The bill of his blue cap hid his eyes, but there was something about the way his eyebrows arched up at the corners . . . . The man swung her around, one hand clamped over her mouth, one forearm pressed against her neck. "Don't scream," he said.

Her instincts kicked in. She slammed him in the rib cage with her elbow. She stomped his instep. When he roared and loosened his grip, she bolted.

1. A clue that Kaitlin ought to begin worrying is placed in the middle of a paragraph. What is that clue? _____

2. Would you guess that Kaitlin has seen her attacker before? _____. Put brackets around the sentence that gives you a clue. Where is that sentence located in the paragraph? _____

3. Circle the sentence that first warns readers that Kaitlin is in real trouble. What is unusual about the placement of that sentence? _____

4. Whisper the words *The bill of his cap* to yourself. The hard consonants might slow you down. Why would the writer want to slow you down right there? _____

☞ A summary is a brief description of the main points of a passage. Summarizing information can help you organize the material in a helpful way. To summarize, decide which information is most important. Organize those important ideas in a logical way. Read the following passage; then answer the questions that ask you to summarize.

Low Tide at Tarawa

On the morning of November 20, 1943, something went terribly wrong in the Pacific Ocean. More than 11,000 U.S. lives were lost as a result. Decades later, astronomy professor Donald Olson figured out what had gone amiss.

The U.S. Marines had planned an assault on Tarawa, a Japanese-held island in the Pacific. An amphibious landing would be best, planners decided. Marines would be transported as close as possible to the beach. The major obstacle was a barrier reef that would have to be crossed. The reef was flat and would support the weight of the LCVPs and LCMs (two types of landing craft) used to transport the Marines, planners thought.

Would tides be high enough to keep the vessels from grounding? Tide tables were consulted. Former residents and shipmasters who had traded in the area were consulted. All indicated that at least four feet of water could be expected at high tide at midmorning on November 20. That would be clearance enough for the fully loaded LCVPs and LCMs, which required three-and-a-half feet of clearance. On the days leading up to the assault, it was observed that the LCVPs and LCMs could run right up to the beach.

The predictions were wrong.

The vessels encountered an unexplained low tide. They grounded at the front edge of the reef. Alligators—landing craft with treads that could move over the reef—had been brought in, but there were not enough. Marines waded chest-deep through the water and were cut down by enemy fire.

What had happened? Donald Olson, a professor at Southwest Texas State University, set out to find out. Who better to solve this mystery than an astronomy professor who could use astronomical analysis and computer simulations? What Olson discovered was that the Marines fell victim to a rare and unforeseen lunar phase. That phase prevented the tides from rising or falling as expected. The predicted high tide had not occurred. This phenomenon occurred only twice in 1943, and the Marines had begun their assault during one of those times.

Olson believes that the discovery of this phenomenon is his most important discovery, but it is not his only one. He also tracked down the spot where the famous photographer Ansel Adams stood while shooting "Moon and Half Dome." He investigated Lincoln's successful defense in a murder trial, based on a question of whether a witness might have been able to observe the nighttime murder.

Not content to stick to the normal investigations of an astronomer, Olson carved out a unique area of expertise for himself. He also managed to clear up a few mysteries along the way.

Write your answers:

1. Write one or two sentences that summarize what casualties the U.S. Marines suffered on the morning of November 20, 1943, at Tarawa. _____

   _____

   _____

2. Write one or two sentences that summarize why those casualties occurred. _____

   _____

   _____

3. Write one or two sentences that summarize the efforts made before November 20, 1943, to be certain that LCVPs and LCMs could clear the barrier reef. _____

   _____

   _____

4. Write one or two sentences that summarize who Donald Olson is._____

   _____

   _____

5. Write one or two sentences that summarize what Donald Olson discovered about Tarawa.

   _____

   _____

   _____

6. Write three or four sentences that summarize this article. _____

   _____

   _____

   _____

   _____

   _____

   _____

   _____

   _____

   _____

☞ Sometimes a reading selection gives you the information you need to make predictions. Read the following selection about forest fires. The questions that follow ask you to make predictions about what might happen in certain circumstances. You will need the information in the article to make those predictions.

Recycled Forests

Animals are born, live, and die. Forests do the same. Most people think that forests are supposed to live forever. Many believe that America was once a great, unbroken forest.

Not so, say some scientists. The North American continent was an open woodland swept by frequent fires. Lightning caused most fires, but volcanoes, sparks from falling stones, and friction from rubbing branches were other natural causes.

What happened after these fires? The land rebounded. Nutrients were returned to the soil. Native grasses and wildflowers such as big bluestem and Indian grass bloomed in meadows opened to sunlight. Insects found homes and food in burned trees. Birds such as woodpeckers enjoyed the new abundance of insect food. Birds of prey feasted on rodents who no longer had as much protective cover, and the rodent population was reduced.

Native Americans understood the benefits of fires. They deliberately set them. When the first European settlers arrived on the North American continent, they saw evidence of these fires. Some described "barrens" or sections of land cleared by Native Americans. Some early European settlers followed the Native American policies of frequent burn-offs.

This practice is more controversial today. When fires burned 800,000 acres of Yellowstone Park in 1988, one senator called the results an "absolute devastation." He and others questioned the park management's decision to allow naturally occurring fires to burn themselves out. More recently, some have questioned the wisdom of prescribed burns practiced by the Missouri chapter of the Nature Conservancy and other private and government organizations. They want all woodland fires stopped.

That may be a dangerous policy, some caution. Frequent burns keep woodlands free of underbrush. In the absence of fire, underbrush grows unchecked. Trees resistant to fire are displaced by trees which burn more easily. These less-resistant trees and the underbrush can fuel devastating fires.

Once a large fire starts, the question of whether to fight it or not may be an academic one. Ronald Wakimoto, a professor of wild-land fire management at the University of Montana, cautions that large wildfires are no easier to control than tornadoes and volcanoes. John Varley, director of Yellowstone Center for Resources, would probably agree. Although 25,000 men and women fought the Yellowstone fire of 1988, he points out that their efforts were unsuccessful. Not until a light snow fell on September 11 was the fire extinguished.

A drive through burned woodlands might silence critics. Millions of seedlings push up from the renewed soils at Yellowstone. In Victoria Glade near St. Louis, Missouri, prescribed burns have been practiced for 20 years. Twelve-inch collared lizards are colonizing the land again. At the Shut-In Mountain Fen preserve in Missouri, 80 endangered snakemouth orchids welcome the sunlight.

Write your answer.

1. Do you predict that forest management officials will soon agree on whether frequent burn-offs are beneficial? _____. What evidence leads you to make this prediction?

    _____

2. What policy do you predict that Yellowstone Park's management will favor?

    _____

    What evidence leads you to make this prediction? _____

    _____

3. What do you predict will happen in dense forests where prescribed burns are not practiced?

    _____

    What evidence leads you to make this prediction? _____

    _____

4. What do you predict will happen if lightning were to start a fire in a forest which had not experienced a burn-off in many years? _____

    _____

    What evidence leads you to make this prediction? _____

    _____

From Lincoln to Washington: Walking D.C.

Your history fair team won a trip to a ceremony in Washington, D.C. On the morning of the ceremony, your group tours the Lincoln Memorial. Somehow you and one of the chaperones get separated from the others. The bus leaves without you. You have 30 minutes to get to the ceremony. Neither of you has money for a cab. A guard gives you the directions and you scribble them down. Read the scribbled directions and mark your path. Put an X where you think the Washington Monument should be.

Start at the drive which circles the Lincoln Memorial. This is Lincoln Memorial Circle. From there, go northeast on Henry Bacon Drive NW for .2 miles.

Go east for .8 miles on US 50 (Constitution Avenue NW).

Turn right on 15th St. NW.

After .2 miles, turn right on Washington Memorial Driveway SW.

Walk .1 miles. The drive will curve to the right.

Congratulations! You have arrived.

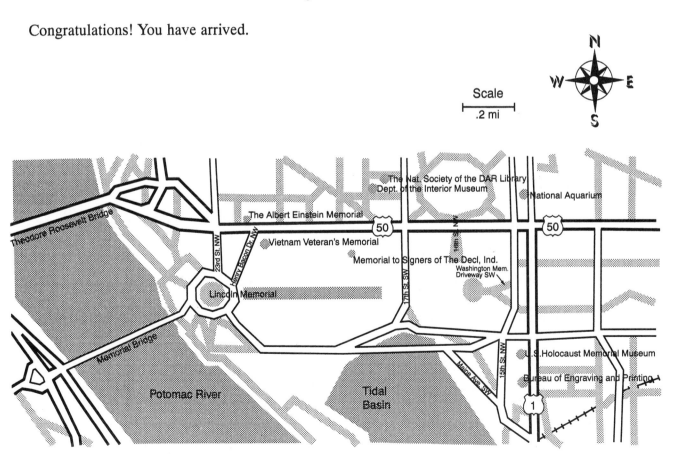

Backups Needed

Ivan stepped back as Grant stomped toward him. "Just back off," Ivan stuttered. "I don't want to fight." But Grant kept coming. Ivan saw one of the boys from his pre-algebra class take one look and then hurry back into the building. Ivan hoped he was going to get one of the APs and that he'd be quick doing it.

This scene includes three characters. Ivan emerges as the main character. Grant is also an important character. What about the third, unnamed character? Could he be left out of the scene? No, this minor character serves a purpose. His reaction confirms that Grant's actions look scary. Ivan doesn't seem to be overreacting.

Sometimes minor characters serve different purposes. They might give a view different from that of the main character, pointing out that the main character could make a different choice. Sometimes minor characters help writers show some important trait of the main character.

Read the passage that follows. Think about what purpose the minor characters serve. Then answer the questions that follow.

Daniel inched closer, until he and Ada were sitting shoulder to shoulder in the empty stands. At the far end of the field, the goalpost cast long shadows across the empty field.

Braver now, Ada smiled up at Daniel. "I thought you didn't like me," she said. "Yesterday when I saw you in the hall, you didn't answer when I said hello."

Daniel took her hand and squeezed it. "I didn't see you. I would never have passed you up if I had." But then he narrowed his eyes and gazed into the distance. When Ada turned to see what had caught his attention, she saw that the track team had burst out of the doors in the athletic hall and were headed down toward the track that circled the football field.

Daniel stood. "I just remembered," he said. "I'm supposed to be at tutorials. My teacher is going to kill me if I'm late."

Before Ada could say anything, he was gone, running down the steps of the stands.

1. Who are the minor characters in this scene? _____

2. What do they show readers? _____

_____

Get a Grip

Best boy, *gaffer*, *dolly grip*—these and other terms scroll across the screen at the end of a movie. Some terms, such as *director*, are clear enough, but others prove more puzzling. What is a *best boy*, for example? Below you will find a few of the most puzzling terms and descriptions of the work these people do.

Don't assume that the best boy is the best behaved of the bunch. The title of best boy is given to the lighting crew member best at supervising the others. The best boy oversees the lighting crew and orders the equipment they will need. Oh, yes—the best "boy" can be a female, too. Male or female, the best boy assists the gaffer.

The gaffer designs the lights. This leader of the lighting crew sets up the lights or orders the others on the lighting crew to do so. Working with the director or the director of photography, the gaffer shapes the set or location so that the lighting works to advantage. This crew leader's title originated from a term first used in European carnivals. In those carnivals gaffers were the people who snagged customers for each attraction and made certain that they were herded inside.

Two titles are drawn from the equipment the crew members use. For example, a dolly is a four-wheeled wagon or cart that guides the camera on a smooth, even track. The dolly grip pushes the dolly. Another piece of equipment on a movie set is the boom. This long, adjustable pole holds a microphone close enough so that voices can be recorded. The boom operator makes certain that the boom does not appear in the camera's view.

The title Foley artist sounds as if it would have something to do with the visual arts, but it does not. A movie's soundtrack is recorded in stages, and one of those stages is the responsibility of the Foley artist. This crew member works in a studio, making sound effects. A Foley artist was responsible for the sounds made when a baby dinosaur hatched in *Jurassic Park*, for example. That artist squeezed an open bottle of dishwater detergent to make the sound. In the days of western movies, Foley artists might have slapped coconut shells against their chests to mimic the sounds of horses clopping along. These days, Foley artists might need computer skills more than they need coconut shells and detergent bottles. More and more sound effects are computer generated.

Foley artists, boom operators, dolly grips, gaffers, and best boys—when you next see a list of credits at the end of a movie, you will have a better idea what these terms mean.

Imagine that your class decides to make an independent film. Some classmates want to work behind the scenes. You need a gaffer, best boy, boom operator, Foley artist, and dolly grip. Read a brief description of these classmates. Based on what you learned on the previous page about the duties of each position, draw conclusions about which classmate will be best for each one.

Sonya: This cheerful classmate likes to be in the middle of whatever is going on but does not want to take center stage. This athletic girl has boundless energy but can sit still for long hours, too. Perhaps her unique combination of athleticism and concentration comes from her career as a competitive gymnast. This girl is strong, but she can move precisely, too.

You have decided that Sonya will be the _____.

Paolo: Known for his attention to detail, Paolo has been class treasurer for three years running. Quiet and thoughtful, he nevertheless always seems to know what is going on. Some of his classmates tease him that he must be psychic, because they swear he knows things that he cannot possibly know. When some of his friends hatched a scheme to prank him, he somehow figured out what they had planned. He caught them in the act.

You have decided that Paolo will be the _____.

Amber: Also known for her attention to detail, Amber is a bit more of a loner than Paolo. She does not like group projects. She will take care of anything she promises to do, and she will do the job right, but just do not ask her to stand around chatting with people.

You have decided that Amber will be the _____.

Angelica: For the last three years, Angelica has studied art both at school and at the Glassell School of Art. She specializes in landscapes, and her professors compliment her for her use of light and color. Although quiet and a bit unconventional in the way she dresses, she is well liked by her classmates. She works well with groups, but she does not like to boss people around. Paolo is her best friend. If there's any bossing to be done, Paolo usually takes care of it for her.

You have decided that Angelica will be the _____.

Lance: Always claiming that he does not understand why the teacher picks on him so much, Lance still does everything he can to annoy her—and most everyone else in the classroom, too. He drops heavy books on the tile floors when everyone is trying to study. He hums. He mimics the sounds of an airplane spiraling down to the ground and crashing. No one can shut him up.

You have decided that Lance will be the _____.

Name _____

Charting a Course for Character Growth

Adventure or outdoor stories prove popular with readers. Careful reading shows you that characters in adventure stories may be doing more than surviving a physical challenge. They may be overcoming some special fear or personality trait. They may be experiencing character growth.

Read the following passages from an adventure story. Some aspect of the main character's personality may be causing him problems. Answer the questions that follow each passage.

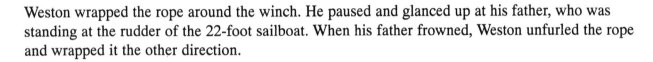

A passage from near the story's opening:

Weston wrapped the rope around the winch. He paused and glanced up at his father, who was standing at the rudder of the 22-foot sailboat. When his father frowned, Weston unfurled the rope and wrapped it the other direction.

"No, no," his father said. "You had it right the first time."

His face flaming, Weston wrapped the rope around the winch the right way, pulled it tight, and secured it to the cleat.

1. Who is the main character? _____

2. What other character is present in this scene? _____

3. What would you guess that Weston will have to learn about himself during the course of this story? _____

_____

A later passage:

Weston's father dove into the water. "Throw me the line," he called, "and I'll tug the boat over to the island. We can tie up there."

Weston did as he was asked, then slumped on the cushions. The sails were luffing, he noticed, billowing in the wind. The wind was catching them, and pushing the boat away from the island.

The sails should be reefed, Weston thought, if his father hoped to tug the boat.

4. Knowing what you know about Weston, is it likely that he will make the decision on his own to tie those sails so that they won't blow in the wind? _____

5. Do you think the action he takes or does not take will make things worse for him and his father? _____

A later passage:
"Weston," his father gasped. "Something's wrong. I must have sprained my shoulder. Help me back into the boat."

One look at his father's face, and Weston knew he had done more than sprained a shoulder. His father's eyes stood out against his pale, pale skin. The skin itself seemed slacker, looser somehow, so that it draped differently across his father's cheekbones.

Heart attack, Weston thought. Or heat stroke. And there wasn't another boat on the lake.

6. What is the main conflict confronting Weston now? _____
_____

7. How is this situation made worse by that trait or fear the writer revealed in the story's opening? _____
_____

8. If the two characters were switched, with Weston in trouble in the water and his father on the boat, would readers feel as much tension? _____

A later passage:
Weston's father had flopped over onto his back. His mouth opened wide as he gasped. Each wave washed water over his face, starting him coughing.

Weston threw a seat cushion into the water, then waited till he was sure his father had grabbed it. Moving quickly, Weston started untying the lines holding the mainsails. He could let the sail drape into the cockpit. That way, the boat wouldn't drift so much when he dived in to help his father.

He heard his father call out, and leaned forward over the railing. "Hold on to the cushion, Dad!" he cried.

"Can't hold on any longer," his father said. "Shoulder's hurting. No time for you to fool with those sails. Jump in and help me get to the ladder."

9. If Weston has not changed any since the beginning of this story, what would he do next?
_____

10. On a separate sheet of paper, write a scene showing how Weston overcomes the fear or shortcoming that caused him problems at the beginning of the story. Show how he struggles and changes in this moment.

Name _____

Test Your SEQ (Self-Esteem Quotient)

Companies, advertising agencies, and even governments conduct surveys. The information gathered from surveys helps companies and governments gauge public interest in a product or policy. Surveys may provide them with information about trends. The products or policies you are offered may depend on the results of the surveys. Reading surveys can help you, too. You can discover information you need or compare your results with those of other respondents.

USA Weekend surveys teens every year. The results are published at their on-line site. Below you will find a section of one of their surveys, as well as results. Cover up the results; then fill in the survey. Compare your results to those of other teens by answering the questions that follow.

1. In general, how do you feel about yourself?
   ____ Really good
   ____ Kind of good
   ____ Not very good
   ____ Bad

2. Which of the following would make you feel better about yourself? (Check all that apply.)
   ____ Getting better grades
   ____ Bulking or toning up
   ____ Losing weight
   ____ Doing better in sports
   ____ Having a better relationship with my parents
   ____ Wearing cooler clothes
   ____ Fitting in with a certain crowd
   ____ Nothing; I like myself the way I am
   ____ Quitting smoking
   ____ Quitting drugs or alcohol

3. Who understands you the most?
   ____ Friend
   ____ Parent
   ____ Boyfriend/girlfriend
   ____ No one
   ____ Sibling
   ____ Religious leader
   ____ Teacher
   ____ Coach
   ____ Other

Here are the results for these questions, gathered from the 272,400 teens who answered the survey:
1. In general, how do you feel about yourself?
    49% Really good
    44% Kind of good
     6% Not very good
     1% Bad

2. Which of the following would make you feel better about yourself? (Check all that apply.)
    49% Getting better grades
    38% Bulking or toning up
    38% Losing weight
    36% Doing better in sports
    30% Having a better relationship with my parents
    24% Wearing cooler clothes
    16% Fitting in with a certain crowd
    15% Nothing; I like myself the way I am
     8% Quitting smoking
     4% Quitting drugs or alcohol

3. Who understands you the most?
    42% Friend
    28% Parent
    10% Boyfriend/girlfriend
     8% No one
     5% Sibling
     1% Religious leader
     1% Teacher
     0% Coach
     5% Other

Write the answers.
1. Only seven percent of teens answered that they felt "not very good" or "bad" about themselves. Compare or contrast your answer to the answer of these teens.

    _____

2. Thirty percent of teens answering the survey reported that they would feel better about themselves if they had a better relationship with their parents. How would your response compare or contrast with that of those teens? _____

3. Fifteen percent of teens do not need anything to make them feel better about themselves. How would you compare or contrast your response to that of these teens? _____

    _____

4. Eight percent of teens answering the survey felt that no one understood them. How would you compare or contrast your response?_____

5. Compare the percentages of teens who thought that getting better grades would make them feel better about themselves to the number who thought that either bulking up or losing weight would make them feel better about themselves. _____

    _____

☞ A passage in a textbook or educational magazine might have a different sound or voice than a passage in a magazine meant to entertain. Word choices might be different. A passage in an educational publication might squeeze more ideas into one sentence. Read the following passage. Think about whether the voice sounds formal or informal. Then answer the questions that follow.

Solar Mysteries

Scientists may have solved one solar mystery while they uncovered a new one. They have long sought an explanation for the Sun's magnetic storms. When they made a discovery that seemed to provide that explanation, a new mystery was revealed.

The Sun's storms are also called *sunspots*. They blast particles into the solar system. Spacecraft are endangered. Communications on the Earth are disrupted. Television and cell phone transmissions are disrupted.

Scientists discovered broad belts of gases. The belts circle the Sun in the mid-latitudes of both the Southern and Northern Hemispheres. They drift down toward the equator. Studying data supplied by the *Soho* spacecraft, scientists were surprised to discover that these bands of hot gases extend at least 12,000 miles below the Sun's surface. Dr. Craig DeForest, a Stanford scientist, compares them to the stripes on a barber pole, except these stripes are circling rapidly. Some may circle at 80 miles an hour. Some move more rapidly than others. Scientists noticed that sunspots were forming at the edges of the bands, where faster-moving bands rubbed against slower-moving ones.

Dr. Douglas Gough, a solar physicist at Cambridge University in England, cautions that scientists cannot yet predict when sunspots will occur. Still, this discovery may offer an explanation for the sunspots, clearing up one mystery.

While scientists were solving this mystery, they uncovered a new one. *Soho*'s data revealed that the entire outer layer of the Sun, down to a depth of at least 15,000 miles, seemed to be sliding from the equator toward the poles. In a little over a year's time, material that started out at the Sun's equator drifted to one of the poles. This flowing of the Sun's outer layer toward the poles is the reverse of the drift of the bands of hot gases.

Scientists are not certain yet of the implications of these new discoveries. One thing is certain— scientists are unlikely to solve all the Sun's mysteries any time soon.

Write your answer.

1. The sentence "While scientists were solving this mystery, they uncovered a new one" includes two ideas. The two ideas are that scientists were solving one mystery and that scientists found a new mystery. How many ideas does the sentence "Spacecraft are endangered" include? _____. The sentence "Scientists noticed that sunspots were forming at the edges of the bands, where faster-moving bands rubbed against slower-moving ones" includes three ideas. What are those ideas? (Write a short sentence or clause for each one.) _____

   _____

   _____

   The sentence "Spacecraft are endangered" occurs near the first of the article. The sentence "Scientists noticed that sunspots were forming at the edges of the bands, where faster-moving bands rubbed against slower-moving ones" occurs near the middle of the article. Which sentence is easier to understand? _____

   _____

   What reason would the writer have for including fewer ideas in sentences near the beginning of the article? _____

   _____

2. Circle any words that you might consider technical or difficult. Underline any contractions or words that you might consider slang. Did you have more circled or underlined words?

   _____

3. Count the number of words in the first paragraph. Divide by the number of sentences in that paragraph. What is the average number of words in each sentence? _____. Do the same for the fifth paragraph. What is the average number of words in each sentence for that paragraph? _____. Writers pay attention to the lengths of their sentences. It is no accident that there is a difference in the average number of words in each sentence. If those differences are deliberate, what could the writer's purpose be? _____

   _____

4. Would you consider this passage most appropriate for an educational publication or for one meant for entertainment? Base your answer on what you have discovered from answering the previous two questions, not on whether the subject interests you.

   _____

Name _____

☞ Passages may contain many details, but you may not need to read all those details. Sometimes you are searching for specific information. The best idea then may be to scan the article for the information you need. To the right, you will find two graphs that show when air-breathing rockets would function normally and when they would switch to air-breathing mode. To decide which graph is correct, you need to know specific details. Scan the article to find the details you need. Underline the sentences that include that information. Then draw a circle around the correct graph.

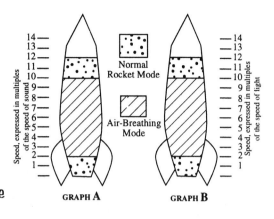

Air-Breathing Rockets

Do you dream of flying into space some day? You may not have to be an astronaut to accomplish your goal. NASA has taken a step toward making space flight possible for ordinary people. It has just completed tests on an air-breathing rocket.

What is an air-breathing rocket and what does it have to do with space travel for ordinary people? Current rockets require liquid oxygen in the fuel mix. An air-breathing rocket would be capable of inhaling some of the needed oxygen from the atmosphere before it thrusts a spacecraft into space. Because less liquid oxygen would be needed, fuel loads would be lighter. Today, fuel weight makes up 85 percent of the total weight of a rocket.

Less fuel weight means less cost to launch a rocket. Uwe Hueter, manager of NASA's Advanced Reusable Technologies, points out that it costs about $10,000 per pound to transport a person into space. He hopes that the air-breathing rockets will reduce the cost to something like $300 per pound. He also hopes that the spacecraft would be reusable—able to take off and land and be readied for travel again a few days later.

Don't reserve your spot just yet. NASA has not built a spacecraft that would use the air-breathing rockets. The two years of tests just completed were ground-based tests. Hueter does know how the rocket is expected to function in flight. It would have two modes—rocket mode and the air-breathing mode. In rocket mode, it would function as a normal rocket would, using stored liquid oxygen to help burn the hydrogen fuel. The spacecraft would take off in this mode. It would shift to the air-breathing mode when the spacecraft was going about twice the speed of sound. Oxygen from the atmosphere would mix with the fuel. The rocket would continue breathing atmospheric oxygen until the spacecraft was going 10 to 12 times the speed of sound. At that point, it would revert back to the rocket mode, blasting into a low Earth orbit.

Does this sound like fun? You had better start saving your money. Even at the relatively cheap cost of $300 per pound, your ticket into space will carry a hefty price tag.

☞ Persuasive writing has a purpose. The writer wants to convince you to take some action or adopt some view. A book report can be persuasive. Below is a book report which includes a mixture of fact and opinion. Read the report. Circle the facts. Underline opinions. Put brackets around any passages which urge you to take some action or adopt a specific view.

An Oldie, But Goodie

"Something moved on the end of the dock. Chris walked quickly toward it, scanning the water on both sides of him. It moved again, slow and colorful, pushed by the gentle breeze . . . Molly's coloring book."

Molly is Chris's little sister. Chris's discovery of her coloring book is the first of the harrowing discoveries he makes in *Someone Was Watching*. Author David Patneaude immerses readers deeply into Chris's viewpoint. He forces readers to experience each rise in tension along with Chris. A must-read for teens, this book grabs readers in the beginning and won't let them go until the last page.

The book is available through Amazon.com. Order it now!

If you were to look for this book on Amazon.com, list three other facts you would like to know before deciding to buy it.

1. _____

2. _____

3. _____

Name _____

☞ When you read, you sometimes spot unfamiliar words. Some of the words in bold type in the passage below might be unfamiliar. Read the passage, think about the topic, and look for other context clues. Answer the questions that follow the passage.

Radioactive Ants

When James Johnson and Paul Blom found ant tunnels in soil at the Idaho National Engineering Laboratory, they knew that they had found trouble. Harvester ants had tunneled into soil covering radioactive wastes. The ants were probably radioactive.

Johnson and Blom found networks of nearly vertical tunnels about the same diameter as a straw. Previous research warned Johnson and Blom that ants could **concentrate** radioactive wastes in their mounds. **Contaminants** could be brought to the surface. Water seeping through the straw-sized tunnels might also be **redistributing** the radioactive wastes.

What could be done? Johnson and Blom needed to find a **biobarrier.** They created four-foot-tall plexiglass ant farms to test various materials. Colored aquarium gravel marked each layer. The deepest layer **represented** the contaminated soil. If they discovered the colored gravel from that layer mixed in with other layers, the ants had broken through the biobarrier.

Johnson and Blom discovered that ants would eventually **breach** a cobblestone barrier. They tested another combination that seemed to work. They used a layer of gravel, more finely grained than the cobble. The layer was 25 cm thick, a little thicker than a mattress, and was placed about 25 cm beneath the surface of the soil. Now they are testing thinner layers. They want to **determine** the thinnest level of gravel that will work.

Their task is **complicated** by another problem. Other burrowing creatures inhabit the arid soil near the laboratory. Rodents such as deer mice can transport radioactive materials away from waste-disposal sites, too. Biobarriers that stop ants may not stop these small rodents, and barriers that work for these rodents may not work for the ants. For example, the cobbles did stop the rodents, but gravel does not seem to work as well.

These complications have not discouraged Johnson and Blom. Perhaps the best biobarrier will be some mixture of cobble and gravel, they reason. They will keep testing materials. They have high hopes. They want to find a biobarrier that will protect radioactive wastes from ants and rodents for the next 500 years.

Circle the best answer.
1. As used in the passage, the word **concentrate** seems to be
   a. noun
   b. verb
   c. conjunction
   d. used incorrectly

© Instructional Fair • TS Denison   111   IF8720 Reading Comprehension

2. Since the passage talks about radioactive wastes, the word **contaminants** probably refers to
   a. pesticide wastes
   b. medical wastes
   c. petroleum by-products
   d. radioactive wastes

3. Since the clause that includes the word **redistributing** comes after a clause that talks about water seeping into the tunnels, you might guess that **redistributing** has something to do with
   a. water washing the wastes into new places
   b. water flooding the tunnels and killing the ants
   c. the rate at which water seeps into the tunnels
   d. the amount of water ants need to survive

4. Since the previous two paragraphs had talked about the need to stop ants from digging into radioactive wastes, the word **biobarrier** probably refers to
   a. an inability to understand anything related to biology
   b. a fear of anything living
   c. a structure or substance that lets living things pass
   d. a structure or substance that keeps living things from passing

For the remaining questions, use some of the context clues you have used in the first four questions to determine the answer.

5. As used in this selection, **represented** means
   a. stood for
   b. distorted
   c. misstated
   d. resented

6. As used in this selection, **breach** means
   a. repair
   b. build
   c. colonize
   d. break through

7. As used in this selection, **determine** means
   a. control
   b. calculate
   c. mean
   d. rule

8. As used in this selection, **complicated** means
   a. bungled
   b. simplified
   c. made worse or more difficult
   d. confused

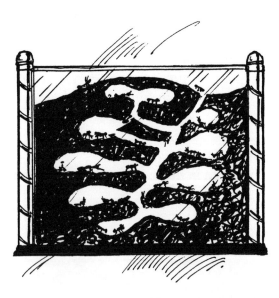

☞ Cheerleaders walk past your group, carrying their megaphones and poms. "Stuck-up snots," your friend says.

When your friends expect all people who look a certain way or are members of a certain group, or who share certain beliefs to behave in a predictable manner, they are stereotyping the people. They are not looking at them as individuals.

Stories and books sometimes include stereotyped characters. Read the following passage. On a separate sheet, list four stereotypes you find.

Who Are These People?

"Mom?" Jen called as she dropped her books on the hall table. "Something terrible happened today." A delicious cinnamon-and-apples scent drifted from the kitchen. The floor gleamed with polish.

"I'm right here," her mother said, coming out of the kitchen. She wiped her hands on her apron. "What's so terrible?" she said, smiling at Jen.

Jen followed her mother into the kitchen, waving to her grandmother, who sat in the rocker in a sunny corner of the kitchen. "We started a unit in algebra," Jen said as her mother took applesauce cookies out of the oven. "I didn't understand a thing the teacher said. Could you help me with my homework when you get through with the cookies?"

"Oh, tonight is my canasta night." Her mother set the cookie sheet down and nodded toward the bay window that looked out over the backyard. "Maybe your brother can help you."

Jen watched her brother and his best friend playing catch for a moment. Then she sighed. "He always punches me in the arm when I don't get the answers right. He's so good in math that he can't understand why it takes me so long to work the problems."

"Maybe your dad can help you when he gets home from the office," Jen's mother said, just as Jen heard a tiny pinging sound. When she looked over at her grandmother, she saw that the old woman had dropped her knitting needle on the floor.

"Here it is, Granny," she said, retrieving the needle.

"You're lucky your grandfather isn't teaching you," Granny said as she took the knitting needle from Jen. "He used to hit the boys with a razor strap when they got their answers wrong."

Jen and her mother exchanged glances. Granny was talking about her own father, not Grandfather. Grandfather had been a kindly soul with twinkling blue eyes. Granny sometimes got things mixed up these days.

Jen let her hand rest on her grandmother's shoulder for a moment. Life was short, she thought. Maybe she shouldn't worry so much about her grades. Maybe she should enjoy herself more, so she'd have lots of pleasant memories when she was an old woman.

"You know what?" she asked her mother. "When Dad comes home, I think I'll ask him to take me shopping instead."

Watch Out

When 13-year-old Ciara's little sister fell into a pail of water, she almost drowned. It was only then that Ciara noticed the warning that read *Children can fall into a bucket and drown. Keep children away from buckets with even a small amount of water.* Now she finds warnings everywhere.

On a hair dryer, she reads:
1. Always unplug after use.
2. Do not place or store where dryer can fall or be pulled into tub, toilet, or sink.
3. Do not use while bathing.
4. Do not use near or place in water.
5. If dryer falls into water, unplug immediately. Do not reach into water.

On a bottle of AHA skin toning lotion, she reads:
Caution: Avoid contact in eyes, on eyelids, on lips and other mucous membranes. For external use only. Keep out of reach of children.

On a car air bag, she reads:
Children 12 and under can be killed by this air bag.
The safest place for children is in the back seat.
Never put a rear-facing child seat in the front seat.
Sit as far back from the air bag as possible.
Always use seat belts and child restraints.

Circle your answers.
1. What is the manufacturer afraid might happen if Ciara were to use the hair dryer while bathing?
   a. The humidity would make her hair frizzy.
   b. The humidity would make the warning decals fall off the dryer.
   c. The humidity would make the wiring rust.
   d. She might drop the dryer into the water and be electrocuted.

2. If Ciara and her little sister argue over who gets to ride in the front seat, and Ciara wins, air-bag manufacturers would probably _____.
   a. suggest she sit as far back as possible
   b. suggest she sit as close to the air bag as possible
   c. be alarmed, since children shouldn't sit in the front seat
   d. not have any suggestions to make

Dogs to the Rescue

A book or article presents information in a linear way. You read down the lines to get the information. A concept map or mind map presents information differently. The main idea is placed in the center. Other ideas that relate to the main idea are placed in bubbles or on rays that move out from the main idea. Ideas that relate to one another are connected by lines or rays. That may make it easier to see how ideas relate. Look at the concept map on the next page; then answer the questions that follow.

1. Why must an SAR (Search and Rescue) dog be from one of the working breeds? _____

   _____

2. Is CPR training required or optional for owner/members of SAR teams? _____

   _____

3. Are special orienteering skills required or optional for SAR team members?

   _____

4. Are basic obedience classes a requirement?_____

5. Does the owner/member of the SAR team have to go through basic obedience training with the dog? _____

6. If an owner was on call with his computer company 24 hours a day to clients, would that owner-and-dog team likely be accepted for SAR training?_____

7. What is main topic of the concept map? _____

8. Read the following passage. Look at the concept map to see what is missing. SAR teams participate in searches for disaster victims, lost children, hunters and hikers, and crime evidence. What others do they search for? _____

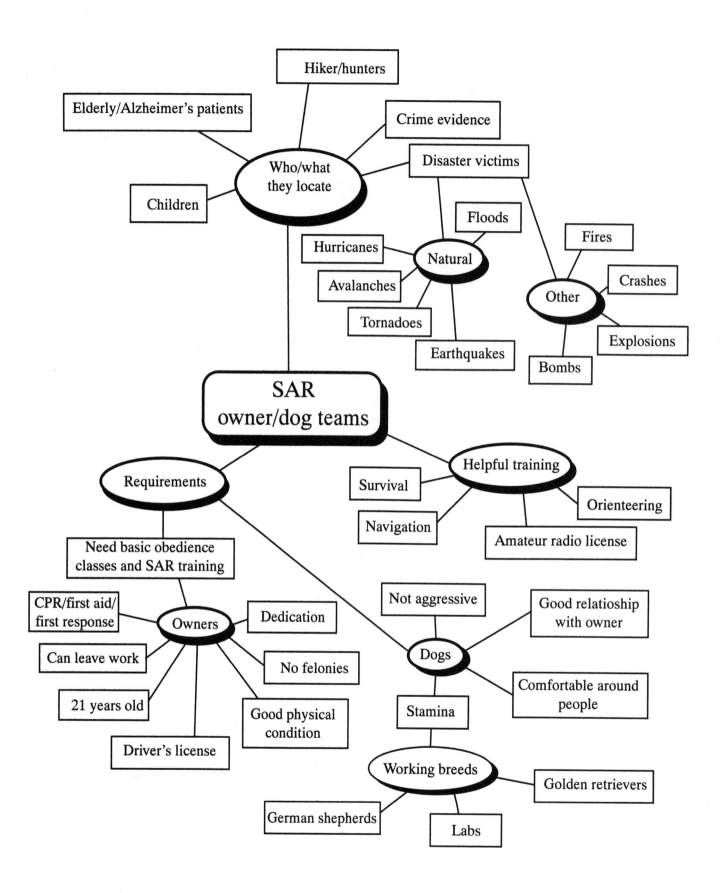

- Hiker/hunters
- Elderly/Alzheimer's patients
- Crime evidence
- Children
- **Who/what they locate**
- Disaster victims
  - **Natural**
    - Floods
    - Hurricanes
    - Avalanches
    - Tornadoes
    - Earthquakes
  - **Other**
    - Fires
    - Crashes
    - Explosions
    - Bombs

SAR owner/dog teams

- **Requirements**
  - Need basic obedience classes and SAR training
  - **Owners**
    - CPR/first aid/first response
    - Dedication
    - Can leave work
    - No felonies
    - 21 years old
    - Good physical condition
    - Driver's license
- **Helpful training**
  - Survival
  - Navigation
  - Orienteering
  - Amateur radio license
- **Dogs**
  - Not aggressive
  - Good relatioship with owner
  - Comfortable around people
  - Stamina
  - **Working breeds**
    - German shepherds
    - Labs
    - Golden retrievers

☞ In the selection below, some of the words in bold type may be unfamiliar. First read the selection. Decide the main idea of the selection. With the main idea in mind, use context clues to help you decide the meanings of the unfamiliar words.

Touching Dinosaurs

Did you ever wonder how a dinosaur's skin would feel? **Paleontologists** with the American Museum of Natural History's expedition to Argentina are finding out. A **calamity** that happened 70 to 90 million years ago is **affording** scientists the opportunity to touch a sauropod's skin.

Actually, the paleontologists are not touching the dinosaur's skin. They are touching a **cast** made of the skin when the sauropod was fossilized. But Luis Chiappe, coleader of the expedition, and the other scientists **collaborating** with him can feel the nubby texture of the tiny, lizard-like scales. They can touch the **impressions** made by the bigger scales that probably ran down the middle of the animal's back.

The cast was discovered when paleontologists **unearthed** a hidden nesting site that contained thousands of six-inch dinosaur eggs. Everywhere the scientists walked across the square-mile site, they stepped on the dark-gray fossil **fragments** of eggs. Along with the shells, they found the first fossilized sauropod embryos ever discovered. Sauropods were the class of plant-eating dinosaurs who had small heads, long necks and tails, and who **lumbered** about on four massive legs.

The discovery of the embryos showed paleontologists how a dinosaur's skin might have felt. The discovery settled a long-fought controversy, too. Some paleontologists had **postulated** that sauropods gave birth to live infants. The presence of the unhatched embryos **verified** that sauropods laid eggs.

One scientist discovered an embryo with 32 teeth, each about two millimeters long. Scientists also discovered that embryos were probably about 15 or 16 inches long when they broke out of the shell. Studying the teeth and other characteristics, paleontologist Rodolfo A. Coria **resolved** that the eggs contained a particular type of sauropod embryos—titanosaur embryos. Titanosaurs were **diminutive** by sauropod standards, growing to only about 45 feet.

It was not as **astounding** to find teeth as it was to find the casts of soft tissues like skin. That any embryos were found at all was a **fortuitous** event for paleontologists. It required that the eggs be covered quickly with a soft silting of sand. Indeed, the eggs were found in finely grained sandstone. What had been a catastrophe for thousands of sauropods near birth was **transformed** many millions of years later into that lucky event for paleontologists—and for the rest of us who would like to know how dinosaur skin felt.

Match the words with their meanings by placing the letter of the correct answer in the blank. Keep the main idea of the selection in mind as you make your choices.

_____ 1. postulated

_____ 2. fragments

_____ 3. affording

_____ 4. paleontologists

_____ 5. astounding

_____ 6. diminutive

_____ 7. fortuitous

_____ 8. calamity

_____ 9. collaborating

_____ 10. unearthed

_____ 11. impressions

_____ 12. lumbered

_____ 13. transformed

_____ 14. cast

_____ 15. verified

_____ 16. resolved

a. indentations

b. changed

c. mold

d. small

e. discovered

f. giving

g. proved

h. determined

i. surprising

j. working cooperatively

k. proposed

l. lucky

m. plodded

n. pieces

o. catastrophe

p. scientists who study fossils

Answer Key

Epidemic   page 2

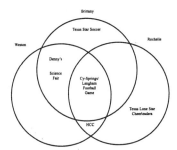

What It's All About?   page 3
1. Home is where the heart is.
2. Beauty is in the eye of the beholder.
3. Believe only half of what you see and nothing that you hear.
4. He who fights and runs away may live to fight another day.

We All Know Lucy, But Who Are Madelyn and Bob?   page 4
writing, episode, recognizable, sitcom, funny, happened, order, scene, contribution, deserved

Help on the Internet   page 6
1. Site 6
2. Site 5
3. Site 3
4. Site 2 and Site 5
5. Site 7

Hunting the Causes of Lightning   page 8
1. They also measure temperature and air pressure.
2. Texas, Oklahoma, Colorado, and Nebraska were the states mentioned as being most affected.
3. Lightning causes fire and electrical damage. Lightning is the number one storm-related killer in the United States.
4. Between 60 and 70 percent of the strikes were positively charged.

You Recognize This Person, Don't You?   page 9
3, 1, 2

Ban Oxygen on Everest   page 10
1. N
2. D
3. N
4. D

One Step at a Time   page 12
1. She is trying out for cheerleading.
2. She worries about everything all at once. Because she thinks of all the things that might go wrong, she is tempted to give up.
3. Tracy has trouble breaking big projects into little steps.
4. Circled: One step at a time, she told herself, but her chest tightened.
   She shook her head. Worry about the tumbling.
   Just go forward, she told herself. Just take the first step.
   One step at a time.
5. Yes. She grins, yells, and runs forward, one step at a time.
6. No. It's more important to say something about breaking big projects into small steps.

Curfew Contract   page 14
Students should initial the contract.
1. N   4. Y
2. N   5. Y
3. Y   6. N

Two violations occurred in October, and one occurred in November. Therefore, the three listed violations have not occurred in the same calendar month.

Scientists Take Aim with AImS Camera   page 15
1. Suzanne Thomassen-Krauss was the source of that information.
2. John Hillman was the source of that information.
   space technology
3. He is speculating.
   He does not have special expertise in the medical field, and the article uses words such as "suggests" and "might."

They're Doing What?   page 16
1. c   4. a (students in warm American clothing)
2. b   5. b
3. c   6. c

Standing My Ground   page 18
1. "That one's easy," Justin said. "You've got the skill. You just don't want the ball bad enough."
2. I felt my face flush. "No, ma'am," I said.
   "Nothing," I said, slipping the strap of my backpack over my shoulder.
3. He blurts out "That's not fair!" and he stands his ground.
4. No. Yes.
5. Yes. Cory punts a piece of paper into the lockers, and Mrs. Irani laughs.

Believe It or Not   pages 19 and 20

1. O	8. O	15. F	22. F	29. F
2. F	9. F	16. O	23. F	30. O
3. F	10. O	17. O	24. F	31. F
4. O	11. F	18. F	25. F	32. O
5. F	12. F	19. F	26. O	33. F
6. F	13. F	20. F	27. F	34. F
7. F	14. O	21. F	28. O	35. F

*4. Weather is prediction based on available data.

What Is It?   page 21
1. b   4. a
2. a   5. b
3. b   6. a

Watch That Attitude   page 22
1. lyrical   3. satirical
2. punchy   4. scholarly

Actual or Outlandish?   page 24
1. Tukwila Fire Lieutenant Dave Ewing is the source.
2. The fire lieutenant was involved in the rescue.
3. Cindy Barrett is the source of the information.
4. Her friend told her about it.
5. Circle: Tukwila Fire Lieutenant Dave Ewing, Thursday, Boeing Field, pilot Mike Warren, two-seater plane, One wheel, 60 feet, two cranes, cherry picker, crane operator, last week's luncheon for women in banking, investment banker Cindy Barrett
6. The second incident, about the man falling off the roof, is the urban legend.
7. & 8. Answers will vary.

Tragedy Leads to New Safeguards   page 25
1. Effect   5. Cause
2. Cause   6. Effect
3. Effect   7. Cause
4. Cause   8. Effect

You Can Kill a Horse But Not a Cadillac page 26

1. Commercial
   broad appeal; Some students may write humor, although this may have been a serious appeal to horse owners.
2. Political
   rhyme, well-liked person, and short
3. Commercial
   sentiment
4. Political
   alliteration and sentiment
5. Political
   sentiment, broad appeal, and "I'm like you."
6. Commercial
   sentiment and short
7. Political
   sentiment and short

Spying on the Spies page 27

a. 1
b. 4
c. 2
d. 5
e. 3

1. SECURITY
2. DOCUMENTS
3. SPY
4. DECODE

Surgery at Sea page 30

1. The race has four legs.
2. The Punta del Este-to-Charleston leg is the shortest.
3. The Punta del Este-to-Charleston leg is the last.
4. The next leg would be the Capetown-to-Auckland leg.
5. The Auckland-to-Punta del Este leg is the third leg of the race.

Boogie Over to Florida page 31

Northern Pacific Railroad's "The Yellowstone Park Line"
Florida East Coast Railway's "Speedway to America's Playground"
Chesapeake and Ohio Railroad's "You'll Sleep Like a Kitten on C and O"
Atchison, Topeka, and Santa Fe Railroad's "The Grand Canyon Line"
Aberdeen and Rockfish Railroad's "The Route of Personal Service"

A Letter Home page 32

1. 18 or 19; He was in high school a year earlier.
2. No. Ray mentioned that she might have seen the event in which he was involved at the movies but did not mention that it might have been shown on television newscasts.
3. During World War II
4. Information about the weather might have given people information about troop movements, since it might have provided clues about where Ray and his fellow shipmates were at the time.

Phone Research page 34

1. Green pages (for city government or library listings)
2. Either InfoAccess or green pages would be an acceptable answer.
3. Yellow Pages
4. InfoAccess
5. The green pages
6. page 121

Whose Voice Is It, Anyway? page 35

1. It gives the flavor of Enrique's voice.
2. It gives the flavor of Aaron's voice.
3. The word *encompass* comes from the writer's voice.
4. Enrique speaks in short sentences, while Aaron speaks in longer sentences.
5. Aaron's voice seems confessional.

Warranty/Disclaimer page 36

1. states
2. guarantees
3. flaws
4. enforceable
5. questions
6. addressed

The Birdmen Are Coming pages 37 and 38

1. d
2. b
3. a
4. b
5. d
6. c
7. d
8. a
9. b
10. c

Staging Your First Job page 39

1. b
2. b
3. Yes. Students might think of several ideas, but one is that people would be more likely to set delivery times when they will be home, so many people might order groceries delivered in the evenings.

Mystery Origami Project page 40

The origami project is a swan.

Select-a-Pet Exercise page 41

Newfoundland, Golden Retriever, Dalmatian, Jack Russell Terrier should be crossed out.

Circled descriptions should include Greyhound—requires little grooming, enjoys exercising outdoors as long as it is not too cold, placid and gentle. Dachshund—smooth coats that require little grooming

Miniature Pinscher—high energy, smooth, hard, clean coat, these dogs need little grooming.

The greyhound has all three traits.

New Beginnings page 44

1. Brenda is the main character.
2. 16
3. 1960
4. Elvis's "Blue Hawaii," the pleated skirt, and just being allowed to wear slacks to school reveal the time period.
5. She is in her bedroom.
6. The chest sits at the foot of her bed. There is a full-length mirror in the room.
7. Brenda has to speak to the school board and ask permission for girls to wear slacks to school.
8. Brenda gets flustered when she doesn't know answers. She is pleading for permission to wear slacks, when she never wears them herself and might not feel committed to this cause.
9. Zack is the main character.
10. high-school age
11. the present
12. Answers may vary, but probably yes.
13. He needs to do well at the next swim meet if he hopes to win a college scholarship.
14. He tends to act without thinking. He is impulsive and headstrong.

Skateboarding: Extreme—and Profitable page 45

1. These are not complete sentences.
2. Those words seem chosen especially to draw the interest of readers and make them wonder what might be dangerous or extreme.
3. The writer uses short sentences.
   The writer also uses surprising or intriguing statements.
4. The article most likely would be about how skateboard manufacturers make a profit.
5. Student answers might differ but might include the statements that the writer addresses teen readers directly by using the word *you*, and also that the article discusses a sport practiced by teens.
6. a

Ka-Thump Goes Your Heart   **page 46**
  a. 2
  b. 1

Keeping Track   **page 48**
  1. No. She needs one more metronidazole tablet.
  2. Yes. Not applicable.
  3. She needs two phenobarbital tablets, one and one-half Baytril tablets, and three metronidazole tablets.
  4. Yes.
  5. Yes, She has been given one too many phenobarbital tablets and one too few metronidazole tablets. Call the vet.

Rafting Iguanas   **page 50**
  1. They are part of the Leeward Islands.
  2. Students might answer north or north-northwest.
  3. No
  4. They most probably would have been swept westward.
  5. No
  6. The two hurricanes that might have carried the iguanas to Anguilla are Luis and Marilyn.

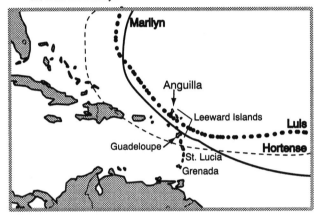

A Better Use for Water   **page 51**
Student answers might differ, but students might include the following points among their three choices: The writer ignores or belittles the need for drinking water. The writer belittles the loss of families' small farms. The writer praises suburban developments as more worthy than farms, and villagers need crops more than they need suburban developments. The writer proposes buying cars to travel to cities to buy water to which the African villagers once had rights. People cannot drink cash, and they need water more than they need cash to buy cars.

Nit-Picking   **page 52**
  1. The birds are seeking an antibiotic substance.
  2. destroying the feathers that insulate them and forcing them to use too much energy to keep themselves warm.
  3. Student answers might differ slightly, but should include the idea that the main topic is that the grooming practices of birds have many purposes.

Coasting Along   **page 54**
  1. T   8. F
  2. F   9. F
  3. F   10. F
  4. T   11. F
  5. T   12. F
  6. F   13. T
  7. T   14. T

Tattoos: Art or Something Else?   **page 56**
Student-drawn concept maps will differ from student to student but should contain almost all details needed to answer the questions on this page.

  1. The overall topic might be listed as tattoos or the social implications of tattoos.
  2. Tattoos probably originated in Egypt.
  3. Slaves, criminals, and aristocrats were all tattooed.
  4. One of the worries is that people with tattoos are antisocial.

Let's Talk About It   **page 57**
  1. Erika is the character who tends to exaggerate.
  2. Simone is this character's name.

Whose Viewpoint Is This?   **page 58**
  1. Student answers might include the following ideas: The writer attends the school. The writer has a best friend named Heather. The writer is not on the newspaper staff. The writer probably is not friends with anyone on the staff.
  2. No. Her friend's all-around gymnastics win was not publicized. Only those students who are on the staff, friends with someone on the staff, or involved in school-sponsored activities can expect to be mentioned, in her view.
  3. No. Students might propose many answers, but some might include the following: Perhaps her friend's accomplishments were not publicized because of a conflict with deadlines. If the writer is not friends with anyone on the staff, she may be assuming that the people publicized are friends with them. She may be speaking out of resentment. She may have a prior conflict with one of the staff members.

Croon a Tune   **page 60**
  1. Student answers might differ slightly but might include the following ideas:
      Infants babble both language and music.
      Infants may have biological cues to develop both language and music.
      Both music and language seem to have biological roots.
      Some language and music skills may be lost if not reinforced early in life.
      Language functions and listening to melodies produce activity in the same part of the brain (the left half).
      All cultures have both language and music.
  2. Student answers might differ slightly but might include the following ideas:
      Some elements of music interpretation are controlled by areas of the brain separate from those that control language.
      Language skills are often reinforced, while musical skills often are not.
      Music skills have been tied to spatial and mathematical skills, while language skills do not have the same kind of ties to spatial and mathematical abilities.
When trained and untrained musicians listen to music, different parts of the brain are most active.

Beep, Beep   **page 62**
Shaniqua: I need to talk to you alone. I need some information.
Gabriela: I'm at home.
Shaniqua: No, no, no. Go to library A.S.A.P.
Gabriela: On my way.
Gabriela: Where are you?
Shaniqua: Plans changed. Transportation problem. I'm at home.
Gabriela: On my way.
Shaniqua: No, no, no. Plans changed. Do not meet me (at) my place. Leaving.
Gabriela: This is getting old.
Shaniqua: I'm sorry. Go home.
Gabriela: I'm mad. You're finished. Attitude adjustment needed.
Shaniqua: Giggle. Happy B-day. Live long and prosper. Go to party. Home.
Gabriela: Laugh out loud. I'm on my way.
Shaniqua: Best friends. Always and forever.

The Integration of Major-League Baseball   **page 63**

1884—"Fleet" Walker's team, the Toledo Blue Stockings, joined the American Association.

1887—The International League stated that no future contracts would be offered to African Americans.

1901—John McGraw tried to sign African-American Charlie Grant (Chief Tokohoma) to his team.

1920s—Jose "Joe" Mendez was considered too dark to be signed.

1927—African-American players travel to Japan.

1933—Babe Ruth and Lou Gehrig traveled to Japan, and the first East-West All-Star game featuring African Americans was played.

1945—Jackie Robinson signed to play on a major-league team.

Creepy Robots   **page 64**

Students might make different choices, due to what they consider "slang" or informal, but they should circle or underline enough words, phrases, or clauses to allow them to conclude that the style is an informal one.

Circled words might include Cool, cool, creepy, creepiest, creepy, or what, isn't, Okay, doesn't, creepy, isn't, Creepy, cool, check it out

Underlined phrases might include your lawn-mowing chores, lets you create your own works of art, so we know what Bay means, us humans, If you would like to know more

1. It might be labeled informal.
2. This would probably be best for a popular magazine.

Candid Camera Kid Still Kids Around   **pages 65 and 66**

1. b   6. d
2. c   7. b
3. c   8. a
4. c   9. d
5. a   10. c

Putting a Best Foot Forward   **page 67**

Answers will vary.

Choco-Raisin-Oatmeal Cookies   **page 69**

Steps in order: 2, 3, 1

The Point of No Return   **page 70**

1. Climax scene
2. Ending
3. Climax scene

Flavorful Speech   **page 71**

1. d   3. b
2. a   4. c

     page 72

1. Chris Thorston
   No
   He seems to be someone who preferred action.
2. Mrs. Marie Hagerty
   This person probably tended to brood over insults.
   Student answers might vary for this question, but may include the idea that this character would find it particularly difficult if placed in a situation in which she was mistrusted or insulted.
3. Alice Caudle
   She would probably rather have been out somewhere.
   This character used the words *a-heap* and *jest*.
4. Joan Didion probably has the most formal education.

Accident Time   **page 74**

1. Dr. Stanley Coren is a neuropsychologist from the University of British Columbia.
2. Alex Vincent is a researcher with Transport Canada.
3. Alex Vincent is the source of this information.
4. Dr. Stanley Coren is the source of this information.
5. Alex Vincent is the source of this information.
6. Dr. Stanley Coren is the source of this information.

7. Alex Vincent is the source of this information.
8. Dr. Stanley Coren studied these collisions.
9. Alex Vincent studied rates for ten years.
10. They obtained different results for the Mondays after Daylight Savings Time ended.
11. Student answers might differ but might include the following ideas: The shorter time period Dr. Stanley Coren studied the rates might not have been as reliable a test of rates. Perhaps rates were lower than normal in those years. Perhaps speed limits changed during the time Alex Vincent studied rates. Perhaps results were calculated or interpreted differently.

Take a Hike   **page 75**

Parentheses should be placed around: don't, we've, won't

Brackets should be placed around: Did your friends make fun of your new shirt? Did your mother make an appointment for you with the dentist you hate? Did your first-period teacher give you a pop quiz? Maybe you ought to take a hike. That dentist you hate? Perhaps you ought to ask her to put a poster on her ceiling. When you take your hike,

Circled phrases: Having a bad day? No, don't run away. Just get outside. Blood pressure lowers. Breathing slows and deepens. That dentist you hate? This theory has a flip side. Scientists call these biophobias. Snakes lurk in rainforests. They won't help your blood pressure.

A Lost Language   **page 76**

1. b
2. b

Discovery Rocks Scientific World   **page 78**

1. O   8. F
2. O   9. F
3. F   10. F
4. F   11. O
5. O   12. F
6. O   13. O
7. F   14. F

Solve the Mystery   **page 79**

The officer probably suspects Matt.

Conflicting Forces   **page 81**

1. She faces conflict due to her teacher's and mother's expectations that she will finish her science fair project on time and conflict about her own tendency to procrastinate.
2. Patrick faces conflict against the other racers and conflict against nature or the weather and its impact on his injury.

Be Sassy!   **page 82**

Students might legitimately circle additional phrases, but at minimum should circle the following phrases:

Sassy Nuñez, the sassy star seen every day on TFUN-TV's *We Are Cool* dance review. a free 30-minute prepaid phonecard, you'll be the center of attention! They'll all be yours, in limited quantities, Call by 5:00 this afternoon

1. No. Student answers might differ here, but the general idea is that the passage might make students feel badly about themselves or feel unworthy.
2. Again, student answers might differ but might include the idea that the advertiser might want consumers to feel so badly about themselves that they will buy the product in order to feel better.

Speaking Out   **page 84**

A. 1, 2   F. 1, 2
B. 2, 1   G. 1, 2
C. 2, 1   H. 2, 1
D. 2, 1   I. 1, 2
E. 2, 1   J. 1, 2

Texas Legend—Subject of Controversy page 86
2. 162 feet
5. 462 feet

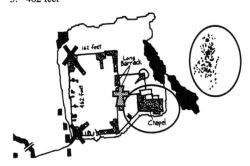

Tell the Truth page 87
1. Josh is the narrator of this passage.
2. No
3. Josh squeezes Ginny's hand, as if he is warning her not to say anything. Also, his friend Carlos seems to believe that he might be capable of wrongdoing.
4. Jonathan Morris is the narrator of this passage.
5. Yes
6. Jonathan tells readers he is trustworthy, and his actions show that he is right. He watches his sister and does not leave her. He makes a note to get medical care for the dog.

Ask the Experts page 88
Student answers will differ but might include the following ideas:
Cuzin
How will nonreflective glass brighten the *Mona Lisa?*
What evidence do you have that cleaning the *Mona Lisa* will harm it?
Are oil-on-wood paintings more difficult to clean than paintings on canvas?

Laing
How effective do you believe the Louvre's plan to use nonreflective glass will be at brightening the *Mona Lisa?*
What evidence do you have that cleaning the *Mona Lisa* would be safe?
Are oil-on-wood paintings more difficult to clean than paintings on canvas?

Silent Calls page 90
1. Graph A gives this information.
2. The absorption rate at 25 Hertz is approximately .02 dB/1,000 feet.
3. Graph B would be most helpful.

High Jumps: High Dreams page 92
1. Alice Coachman grew up in the '30s, and her family probably did not have much money for luxuries.
2. Alice Coachman grew up in a time when girls were expected to behave differently than boys. Alice Coachman probably also grew up in a family that spanked.
3. Students might infer either that the Olympics were not held, or the more imaginative students might infer that Alice Coachman served in the Armed Forces and so could not participate. Although that did not happen, it might be a legitimate inference for them to make.
4. During the World War II years, Alice Coachman was probably stronger or swifter than she was at age 25.
5. Segregation was probably in effect in Albany at that time.
6. No, students are not provided with enough information to make this inference.
7. No. An African-American girl might not have been allowed to participate at that time.

It's a Wash page 93
1. A stain might not have been treated before washing. The top might have been washed with dark blue clothes. It could be fabric softener residue.

2. The khakis might have been washed with towels, or paper or tissues might have been in the pockets.
3. The National Honor Society pin was not removed before the shirt was washed.
4. The rayon shirt was probably dry clean only.

Don't Scream page 94
1. Kaitlin heard a branch snap.
2. Yes. It is located in the middle of the paragraph. Place in brackets: The bill of his blue cap hid his eyes, but there was something about the way his eyebrows arched up at the corners . . . .
3. Circle: Until she glanced back over her shoulder. It is placed by itself in a single-sentence paragraph.
4. The writer wants the reader to notice the clues in that sentence.

Low Tide at Tarawa page 96
1. The Marines lost 11,000 people the morning of November 20, 1943.
2. An unexplained low tide kept the LCVPs and LCMs from running all the way to the beach. The Marines had to wade in and were cut down.
3. Tide tables and former residents and shipmasters were consulted. Tests were conducted, and they showed that the LCVPs and LCMs could go up to the beach.
4. Donald Olson is an astronomy professor who also investigates astronomical mysteries in history, literature, or the arts.
5. Donald Olson discovered an unforeseen lunar phase that prevents tides from rising or falling. This phase stopped the expected high tide the morning of the invasion.
6. On November 20, 1943, the U.S. Marines invaded Tarawa. They encountered unexplained low tides that grounded them, resulting in 11,000 lost U.S. lives. Donald Olson, an astronomy professor at Southwest Texas State University, investigated and discovered that a rare and unforeseen lunar phase was responsible for the unexplained low tide.

Recycled Forests page 98
1. No. The article makes it clear that the controversy over how to manage fires has persisted at least since 1988 and has not yet been resolved.
2. Yellowstone Park's management will probably continue to favor a policy of allowing fires to burn themselves out.
   The 1988 fire was allowed to burn itself out, and the article points out the benefits to the park. John Varley is quoted as saying that firefighters were not successful in putting out that fire anyway and that only a snowfall put it out. This seems to predict that park management does not feel that fighting a large fire would be successful and that there are benefits to a burn-off.
3. Underbrush will grow heavier. Trees that are not resistant to fires will grow.
   Several statements in this article point to this possibility. One statement early in the passage points out that there was no longer as much protective cover after the Yellowstone fire, so it can be assumed that before the fire, there was more underbrush. Also, one paragraph mentions specifically that underbrush would grow heavier and that trees resistant to fire would be replaced by those that are not resistant.
4. A devastating fire would occur.
   A statement in the article says specifically that devastating fire might occur, but also the fact that 800,000 acres were burned in a single fire in Yellowstone indicates that this is a possibility.

From Lincoln to Washington: Walking D.C. page 99

Backups Needed   page 100
1. The members of the track team are the minor characters.
2. They show readers that Daniel is ashamed to be seen with Ada.

Get a Grip   page 102
Sonya—dolly grip, Paolo—best boy, Amber—boom operator, Angelica—gaffer, Lance—Foley artist

Charting a Course for Character Growth   page 103
1. Weston is the main character.
2. Weston's father is also in the scene.
3. Students might have different answers for this question, but their answers should include the idea that Weston needs to learn to have more confidence, to trust his own judgment, or to feel less embarrassed over minor mistakes.
4. No, it is not likely.

       page 104
5. Yes, his inaction will probably make things worse.
6. Weston's main conflict is saving his father.
7. In order to save his father, Weston must make important decisions, and Weston does not trust himself to make those decisions.
8. No, they would not.
9. He would jump in.

Test Your SEQ (Self-Esteem Quotient)   page 105
Student responses will vary.

       page 106
Student responses will differ for the first four questions, depending on the responses they gave on the student survey on the previous page.
5. More teens thought they would feel better about themselves if they got better grades than thought they would feel better if they bulked up or lost weight.

Solar Mysteries   page 108
1. One. Scientists noticed sunspots. The sunspots were forming at the edge of the bands. At the edge of the bands, faster-moving bands rubbed against slower-moving ones.
   The sentence "Spacecraft are endangered" is easier to understand. Student answers might differ but may include the thought that the writer is trying to hook the reader at the beginning of the article, so is making certain that the early sentences are easy to read.
2. Students will circle different words, depending on their reading ability, but should have more circled words.
3. 13, 21, Students might give different answers, but their answers should again include the idea that the writer wants to hook readers at the beginning, so makes it as easy as possible for the reader to get involved in the article and to read further.
4. This passage would probably be more appropriate for an educational publication.

Air-Breathing Rockets   page 109
Students should circle Graph A, the graph that shows the mode of the rocket in relationship to its speed, expressed in multiples of the speed of sound.

An Oldie, But Goodie   page 110
Facts circled: Molly is Chris's little sister. Chris's discovery of her coloring book is the first of the harrowing discoveries. *Someone Was Watching.* Author David Patneaude. The book is available through Amazon.com.
Opinions underlined: immerses readers deeply into Chris's viewpoint, He forces readers to experience each rise in tension along with Chris. A must-read for teens, book grabs readers in the beginning and won't let them go until the last page.
Phrases bracketed: Order it now!

Student answers will differ, but might include the following ideas:
How much does the book cost?
How long or how many pages is the book?
How old is Chris, the main character?
Who are the other important characters in the book?
What is the setting for this book, or where does the book take place?

Radioactive Ants   pages 111 and 112
1. b   5. a
2. d   6. d
3. a   7. b
4. d   8. c

Who Are These People?   page 113
Stereotypes include the following or any combination of the following:
a mom who stays home and bakes cookies and who plays canasta
a forgetful grandmother who sits in a rocker and knits
a two-parent family in which only the father works
an adolescent girl who is not good at math and who likes to shop
an adolescent boy who is good at math and baseball and who teases his sister by punching her
a kind grandfather with twinkling blue eyes
a mean old man who beat his children with a razor strap

Watch Out   page 114
1. d
2. a

Dogs to the Rescue   page 115
1. An SAR dog must have stamina, and the working breeds have stamina.
2. This training is required.
3. This training is optional.
4. Yes, these classes are a requirement.
5. Yes, the owner/member has to go through basic obedience training with the dog.
6. No, this team probably would not be accepted.
7. The main topic is SAR owner/dog teams.
8. They also look for elderly people and Alzheimer's patients.

Touching Dinosaurs   page 118
1. k   9. j
2. n   10. e
3. f   11. a
4. p   12. m
5. i   13. b
6. d   14. c
7. l   15. g
8. o   16. h